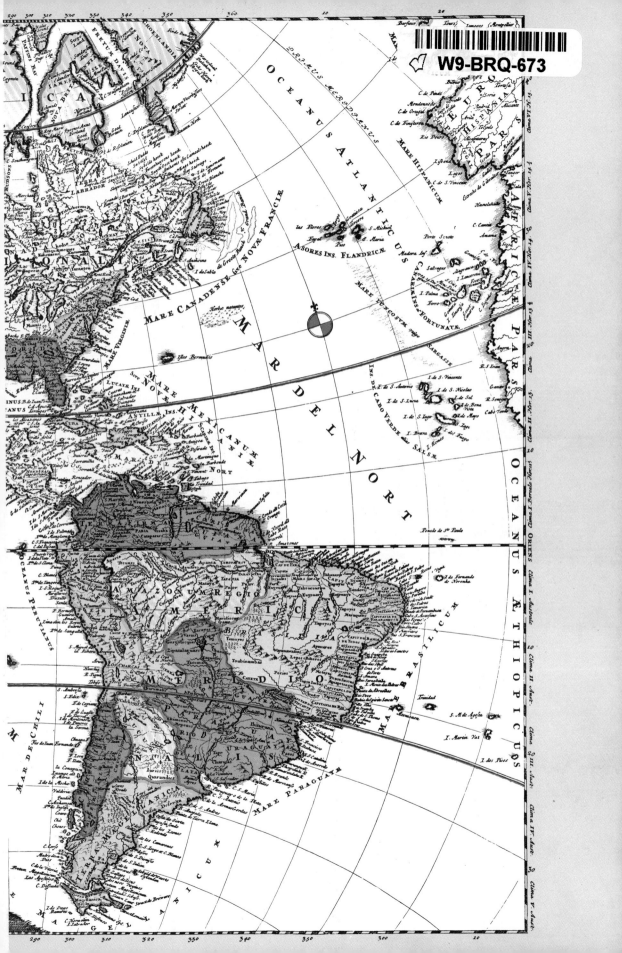

Profile

of

AMERICAN
HISTORY

by

May McNeer

*Happy Birthday
1967
Carla & Pamela*

C. S. Hammond & Company
Maplewood, New Jersey

Other Titles in the PROFILE Series

Cooke: Atlas of the Presidents

Crouthers: Flags of American History

Illustrated Atlas for Young America

Copyright © 1964 C. S. Hammond & Company
Maplewood, New Jersey
Library of Congress Catalog Card Number 64-25037
Printed in U.S.A.
Reproduction in whole or in part
prohibited without written permission
from the publisher.
Designed by Isabelle Reid

CONTENTS

MAN LEARNS TO ROAM

A man is a wanderer! He is a searcher! Before history began early man moved south as great ice sheets pushed down from the north, covering much of Asia, Europe, and North America. When an Ice Age ended glaciers melted, the weather grew warmer and man slowly went north again. Land bridges were left between continents. Men lived with women and children in caves. To the early man, thousands of years ago, the earth was only as much as he could see around him. The world was a very small size in his mind.

He was so small himself compared to a mammoth — a whale — a saber-toothed tiger! Yet he could kill these huge beasts with his stone weapons. Man traveled from place to place because he needed food. He moved with the seasons to gather wild seeds and berries. He followed animals for hunting. He fled before an enemy. When food grew scarce in his small world he had to go to another. Animals around him also felt hunger, fear, and sometimes, even curiosity. But only a human being knew that he wanted a better life. Only he believed in gods and religion. Only man could laugh. He discovered fire, and made tools as well as weapons. Only a man, woman, or child could wish to know what was just beyond his sight.

A man noticed that logs floated downstream, and tossed along on rolling ocean swells. He made rafts of logs lashed together, and rode on them. He found that animal skins would float if blown up. He clung to these and pushed with his feet to move on. He crossed rivers in baskets made of rushes and mud, and he carved logs into canoes. He had paddles, poles, and oars to speed the journey. In time he improvised sails, and learned to make use of the winds to skim him over the waters.

From the Polynesian islands of the Pacific Ocean men of Samoa and Tahiti built outrigger canoes big enough to carry a hundred people and their food and water. They sailed great distances, using only their memories and their knowledge of sun, moon, stars, winds, and waters to guide them.

Only after men had invented tools to shape planks and make keels for their ships could they extend their

☆ 9

trading with others in distant lands. Probably the earliest ships were launched on the River Nile, in Egypt. Egyptians, men from the island of Crete, and Phoenicians traded across the Mediterranean Sea. Then hardy sailors of Phoenicia, the land of Lebanon, ventured past the Rock of Gibraltar into the Atlantic Ocean. Greeks and Romans were daring seafarers also. Ships became fighting galleys and Romans called the Mediterranean *Mare Nostrum* — "Our Sea." They built ships with rounded bows. By the time that Viking ships were cleaving icy waters in the north Arab vessels from Basra, on the Persian Gulf, were trading in the Indian Ocean and with the Spice Islands.

Men wandered on the land also, hunting game and different foods. Bands of men went out to conquer other peoples. Whole groups or tribes traveled to escape invaders of their home grounds. Or a man might take his family beyond the horizon because he was adventurous in spirit!

Over a period of centuries men learned that animals could be tamed and used to carry loads. In Asia the slow-footed camel took on this burden. The elephant and the water buffalo carried people and goods. Donkeys were loaded and swift horses were trained for men to ride. With the invention of the wheel a man could make an animal pull a cart. It was the wheel that started mankind on a road to a different life!

The domesticated animal and the wheel moved men from place to place at a faster speed. Yet they also helped him to settle in one home after he had learned to grow food. He had a cart, a waterwheel, a grindstone. Man's sense of adventure and his wish to get more pushed him forward on wheels. Trading and warfare drove him onward. Wheels and ships carried him forward on his way to progress.

A man's thoughts about the world changed as he moved faster and farther to more distant places. His understanding of time was different now. Once early man had thought of time as the space from sunrise to sunset — and season to season. Now he thought of time as years. It took several years to voyage around Africa to the East Indies and return.

Most men still believed the earth to be flat. The size of the earth was small and the shape unknown to him even with his new knowledge. Yet daring sailors wondered what was out there at the rim of the world. Undoubtedly the Atlantic Ocean was swarming with strange serpents, mermaids, monsters and gigantic waterspouts shooting up from the noses of giant leviathans! A sailor wouldn't venture westward without a brave spirit and a strong reason.

ADVENTURE BY SEA AND LAND

Long before any seaman in Europe had the courage to sail due west to the unknown there were small groups of people slowly moving eastward. They lived in Asia, and they left no records for they could not read or write. Scientists believe that Stone Age men, women, and children probably crossed over a strip of land that once connected Siberia and Alaska at the Bering Sea. Anthropologists studying fossil bones by measuring the radioactivity of carbon think that they came perhaps twenty thousand years ago.

These Asiatic people carried stone clubs and spears, to fight enormous hairy elephants, sloths, and bison of immense size. They came at different times, in waves of slow movement. Centuries later some of them were in Mexico. Others went all the way to the tip of South America. After a long time groups had moved across North America. They were living in the northern forests, in the jungles of Florida, in the mountains, and along streams throughout the land.

There were no other peoples on the continent but these tribes when a bold Viking called Leif Ericsson landed on the North American coast. Vikings were Norsemen, and in France and England coastal villagers prayed, "From the fury of the Norsemen, may the good Lord deliver us!" Living in Scandinavia among mountains covered with dense forests, Vikings sailed from their fjords, or inlets, to the sea for plunder and adventure. Their ships were fast and strong, with square sails, and high carved prows, decorated in brilliant colors. Norse sailors manned their vessels with great skill, and when the wind dropped they made use of their trusty oars.

In the ninth and tenth centuries Viking marauders were feared along the Atlantic coasts of France and Spain, and around into the Mediterranean to Italy, as well as in the British Isles. They also penetrated inland waters to make raids in Germany and in Russia. It is believed that Dublin, in Ireland, was founded by the Vikings, who established permanent settlements from which to sweep out across the seas. Iceland was colonized by these daring men from Scandinavia.

Leif Ericsson, son of Eric the Red, who had discovered Greenland in 982, sailed westward toward North America. He was on his way to Greenland to proclaim Christianity for King Olaf of Norway. A great storm came up and tossed the sturdy Viking ship out of its course westward. When the Norsemen came at last to a green coast they went ashore and found wild grapevines bearing sweet fruit. This land, which was probably a part of the New England coast, was called Vineland the Good by Leif Ericsson.

His adventures were written in the ancient Icelandic saga of Eric the Red. Later other Norsemen voyaged to the continent, and legend says that the wife of one of them bore a son, Snorri, who was the first white child born in North America. In recent times pieces of Viking-type weapons have been found as far inland as the Great Lakes region, but how they came there, and when, is a mystery.

Nearly three hundred years later Europeans still did not know that North America existed. All but a few thought the world flat. Nevertheless, there were merchants in Venice who knew that to the east there was a fabulous, jeweled Orient. Two of these merchants were Niccolò and Maffeo Polo. They had traveled overland to India and China, crossing mountains, plains, and deserts. They had seen people and places such as no other Europeans had ever looked upon.

Niccolò and Maffeo Polo's first trip to Cathay, as China was called, had kept them away from home for fifteen years. On their second journey, in the year 1271, they took Niccolò's seventeen-year-old son, Marco, with them. The Pope gave them gifts to take to the Great Khan and sent two priests along to convert the Chinese. Before the Polos had left Armenia, however, the priests grew frightened and returned to Rome. Marco set his eager eyes to looking at strange sights and learning all that he could. These travelers, in their loose, wide coats and little round hats, rode camels and horses, voyaged on ships, and sometimes went on foot. They crossed Arabia and traveled along the coast of Persia to the steppes of Central Asia. Everywhere they traded and made friends. At last they came to the palaces of the mighty Kublai Khan, ruler of the vast and mysterious realm of Cathay.

The Khan received them with joy and gave them rich clothing. He had welcomed Niccolò and Maffeo years before. Now he was warm in his greeting to young Marco. Marco Polo was soon invited to enter the service of Kublai Khan. He remained in China almost twenty years. The Khan made him governor of a great city, and Marco became fabulously wealthy. He accompanied his patron on hunting trips, riding in a richly decorated palanquin atop an elephant. He was sent on important missions to distant walled cities. The three Polo merchants lived like princes in Cathay, but after a while they began to long for the canals and palaces of Venice.

They begged the emperor to let them go. He consented and sent them away with a party bound for Persia. They went on to Constantinople and then home to Venice. In 1295 three oddly dressed strangers appeared at the Polo family palace. When they said that they were Niccolò, Maffeo, and Marco nobody believed them. At last, however, they were permitted to enter.

They stepped to a large table and from hidden pockets poured out a glittering stream of diamonds, pearls, rubies, and emeralds. The staring relatives gasped, and then nodded to each other. These could be none other than Niccolò, Maffeo and Marco! Only friends of the Great Khan could own such gems!

Some years later Marco told to a scribe the story of his journeys and life in the court of Kublai Khan. A book was handprinted in Latin. For centuries *The Adventures of Marco Polo* was a favorite with adventurous men. It sent travelers eastward by the long way. Marco Polo was the first European to trace a route across Asia, and to describe the mysterious kingdoms of the east. He made known several important inventions. Printing from a wood block, gunpowder, and the mariner's compass came to Europe from Asia because Marco Polo first started other Europeans eastward. He was called "Marco Millioni," or "Marco Millions" by his fellow Venetians.

After 1453 merchants of Venice and other cities were cut off from trade with the east. Constantinople fell to the Turks, who swept out of Asia on swift horses, descending on Christians in fierce fighting hordes. The two great opposing powers of that time were Christianity and Mohammedanism. Turkish Mohammedans became a wall to keep merchants from land routes to Asia. Not many camel caravans loaded with Oriental goods could slip through Mohammedan territory safely.

Portugal faced the Atlantic Ocean, and her ruler King Henry, known as Henry the Navigator, chose the sea routes to Asia. Portuguese seamen were daring and skilled. They discovered the Azores and claimed the islands for their King. Portuguese vessels rounded Africa to the eastern lands of spice and gold. These voyages took years. By now trade routes to Europe through the Near East were almost closed. Europe was poor and needed goods. The black plague swept through town after town, and country after country, bringing starvation and death. In the fifteenth century even kings, nobles, and barons were so desperate for money that many became robbers on the highways or attacked the castles of other nobles. Peasants and townsmen, crazed by hunger, rioted in towns as well as in the countryside.

A shorter way must be found to reach the Orient! Then the printing press was invented in Germany by Johann Gutenberg, and *The Adventures of Marco Polo* was circulated in print in 1477. In the port city of Genoa, a seafaring man with some odd ideas got hold of a copy. It left him on fire with excitement. His name was Christopher Columbus.

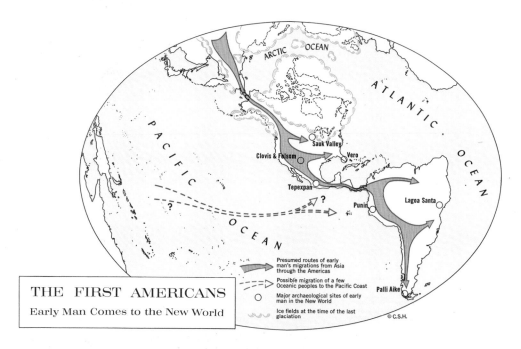

THE FIRST AMERICANS
Early Man Comes to the New World

Presumed routes of early man's migrations from Asia through the Americas

Possible migration of a few Oceanic peoples to the Pacific Coast

Major archaeological sites of early man in the New World

Ice fields at the time of the last glaciation

Indians came to America from Asia more than 20,000 years ago. The first groups were probably hunters searching for game. They crossed the Bering Strait and found their way through the gaps in the retreating glaciers. Others followed at later times, moving slowly southward across the two continents. Archaeologists have found traces of early man in western United States that date back to 15,000 B.C. Remains found at the tip of South America indicate that Indians lived in that remote land more than 8,000 years ago.

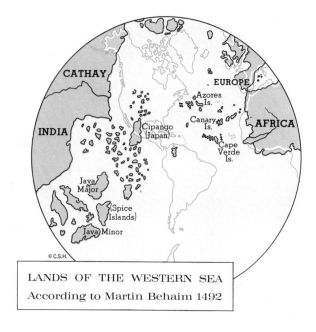

LANDS OF THE WESTERN SEA
According to Martin Behaim 1492

In 1492, Martin Behaim constructed a globe in Nuremberg, Germany that still survives to show us the state of geographical knowledge as it was on the eve of Columbus' first voyage. The map of the western hemisphere, at the left, is based on Behaim's globe. True shapes of the land areas as known today are shown in white outline. Behaim, like other geographers of his day, greatly underestimated the distance from Europe westward to Asia. Behaim's idea of Africa and Europe is roughly the same as the true coastline of these continents. However, the east coast of Asia is inaccurate and is misplaced by a third of the distance around the globe. Of course, neither Behaim nor Columbus knew of the American continents that blocked direct passage across the western sea to Asia.

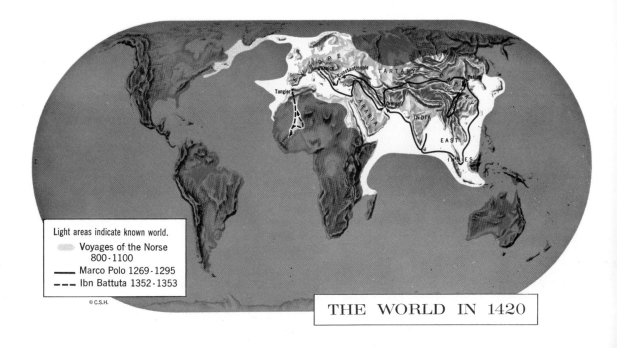

Light areas indicate known world.

▓ Voyages of the Norse
    800-1100
—— Marco Polo 1269-1295
- - - Ibn Battuta 1352-1353

© C.S.H.

THE WORLD IN 1420

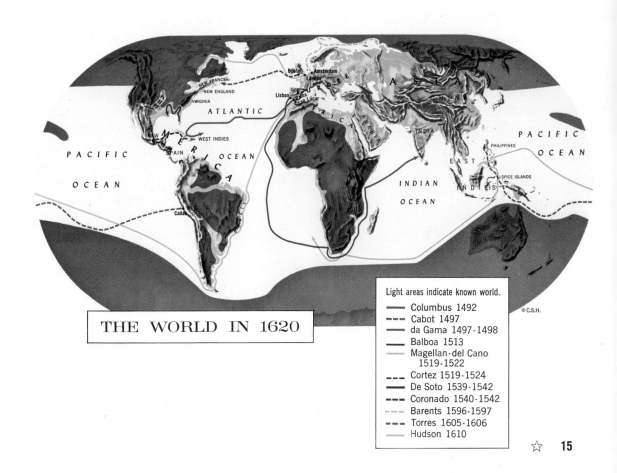

THE WORLD IN 1620

Light areas indicate known world.

—— Columbus 1492
- - - Cabot 1497
—— da Gama 1497-1498
—— Balboa 1513
—— Magellan-del Cano
    1519-1522
- - - Cortez 1519-1524
—— De Soto 1539-1542
- - - Coronado 1540-1542
- - - Barents 1596-1597
- - - Torres 1605-1606
—— Hudson 1610

© C.S.H.

☆ **15**

WEST TO THE UNKNOWN

2

Once ferocious Moorish warriors had overrun Spain. For seven centuries they had held the country behind the Rock of Gibraltar. Then Isabella of Castile had married Ferdinand of Aragon and united their two kingdoms. By 1492 these monarchs had driven the Moors back to North Africa. Now they wanted to rival Portugal on the seas. They listened carefully to an Italian sea captain who believed that the world was round, and that he could sail west to reach the Orient.

The sun was only a pale promise in the sky when voices echoed in the streets of Palos. "The Genoese captain sails today." "Westward?" Sailors shook their heads, "I wouldn't ship out with him. His men will be eaten by monsters of the deep."

Three small vessels floated down the river and caught a fair breeze to the Canary Islands. Then the *Niña*, the *Pinta* and the *Santa Maria* weighed anchor for the first voyage into this uncharted ocean. Their captain-general Columbus fixed his eyes on the west, where he expected to find the lands of India and China. He gave out the course to the flotilla, "West —

nothing north — nothing south."

The *Santa Maria* flagship sped along with a curl of foam at her bow.

The voyage grew long. The three caravels were becalmed in the Sargasso Sea. They were shut in by golden plant life without roots, floating as far as the eye could look. "This must be shallow water!" And yet when leadsmen took soundings they found no bottom. Sailors tried to "whistle up a wind," but no breeze stirred the limp canvas. And then, when they were in despair, they saw their sails catch the trade winds. Now they swung along, leaving three white foamy wakes under the stars. Still they did not come to the shores of India.

The crew grumbled and began to grow mutinous, wanting to turn back. But Captain Columbus persuaded them to go on for just a little while longer. More than once the lookout thought that he saw a misty line of land. It was only a low bank of cloud on the horizon. And then, early in October, huge flocks of birds winged past them. Columbus, knowing that this was a migration to the southwest, followed the flocks instead of his charts.

The crews rushed to the rails, pointing down, laughing, and shouting. Could that be a tree branch floating past them, trailing green leaves and blossoms?

"Land ho! Land! Land ho!"

The lookout on the *Pinta* caught the first glimpse. A cannon boomed the signal to the flagship and the *Niña*. Next day the little caravels dropped anchors off the shore of San Salvador, one of the Bahama Islands. Columbus and his two captains planted the banner of Spain and the cross of Christianity on the white sands.

Believing that he was, at last, in India, Christopher Columbus called the terrified natives Indians. For three months his ships sailed among the islands, searching for the riches and the palaces of the Great Khan of Cathay. Then Columbus returned to Spain. Later he made other voyages to the West Indies, but he did not bring back treasures for Queen Isabella and King Ferdinand. He died not long after his last voyage, still believing that he had found Asia.

The New World was named, not for its discoverer, but for Amerigo Vespucci, who sailed to South America in 1499 and then wrote about it. The thirty-three day voyage of Columbus, ending at San Salvador, was the greatest sea venture of discovery in history. Columbus led the way to western lands, and his voyages established Spain as a rival to Portugal in seafaring discovery.

While in the service of Portugal in 1511 Ferdinand Magellan sailed westward around Africa to the Moluccas, called Spice Islands. He ventured as far as the meridian in which the Philip-

pine Islands are located. By 1519, Captain Magellan was sailing for Spain. He knew that Balboa had stood on a mountain top on the Isthmus of Panama and looked out on an unknown sea. Magellan determined to find a passage around South America to the Spice Islands. With a fleet of five ships he explored the coast until he reached the bleak Straits of Magellan at Cape Horn. Here wild winds tossed huge waves against the rocky shores. Against orders one ship turned back. Another sank under mountainous seas with all souls lost. Three came, battered and broken, into sunny blue waters, which the captain named the Pacific Ocean. He believed it to be, as it was pictured on all maps, a narrow passage called the Great South Seas.

After a long voyage that brought all hands close to starvation, the three ships found the island of Guam. Here natives swarming aboard took away so much with them that Magellan called the islands the Ladrones, or Thieves. Not long after leaving Guam the hardy captain brought his ships to anchor at the island of Samar in the Philippines. By sailing to the west he had reached the same longitude that he had visited some years before. He had circumnavigated the earth, but he was not to go home to tell about it. Magellan was slain by natives of the island of Mactan. Only one of his ships returned to home port in Spain.

Other captains on other vessels found routes to the New World over northern waters. Beginning with John Cabot, who claimed Greenland, Labrador, and Newfoundland for the King of England, captains ventured out to the west for four hundred years looking

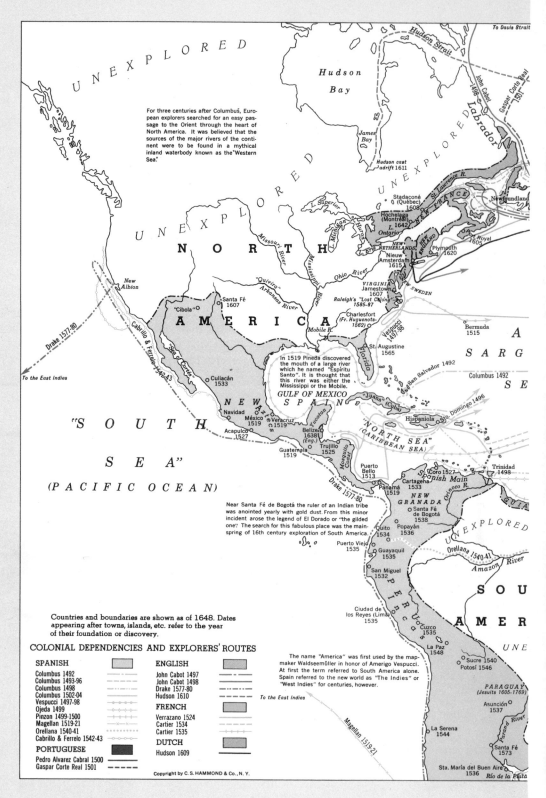

U N E X P L O R E D

Hudson Bay

For three centuries after Columbus, European explorers searched for an easy passage to the Orient through the heart of North America. It was believed that the sources of the major rivers of the continent were to be found in a mythical inland waterbody known as the "Western Sea."

James Bay

U N E X P L O R E D

Hudson cast adrift 1611

U N E X P L O R E D

To Davis Strait

Labrador

Gaspar Corte Real 1501

John Cabot 1498 1497

Stadaconé (Québec) 1608
Hochelaga (Montréal)
St. Lawrence R.
N E W F R A N C E
L. 1642

Newfoundland

U N E X P L O R E D

N O R T H

L. Superior
L. Michigan
Huron
L. Ontario
Erie

Missouri River
Mississippi
Ohio River

NEW NETHERLANDS
Nieuw Amsterdam 1615
NEW ENGLAND
Plymouth 1620
Fr. Royal 1605

A M E R I C A

"Quivira"
Arkansas River

Santa Fé 1607
"Cibola"

Mobile R.

VIRGINIA
Jamestown 1607
Raleigh's "Lost Colony" 1585-87
Charlesfort (Fr. Huguenots 1562)
Vespucci 1497-98
NEW SWEDEN

Bermuda 1515

A
S A R G
S E

Drake 1577-80

New Albion

Cabrillo & Ferrelo 1542-43

Sea of Cortés

To the East Indies

Culiacán 1533

N E W
Navidad
México 1519
Acapulco 1527

Veracruz 1519
Yucatán
Belize 1638 (Eng.)
Guatemala 1519

In 1519 Pineda discovered the mouth of a large river which he named "Espíritu Santo". It is thought that this river was either the Mississippi or the Mobile.

GULF OF MEXICO
S P A I N

Florida
St. Augustine 1565

San Salvador 1492
Columbus 1492

"Juana" (Cuba)
Hispaniola
Sto. Domingo 1496

"NORTH SEA"
(CARIBBEAN SEA)

" S O U T H

S E A "

(P A C I F I C   O C E A N)

Trujillo 1525
Mosquito Coast
Puerto Bello 1513
Panamá 1519

Coro 1527
Cartagena 1533
Spanish Main
Orinoco R.
Trinidad 1498

GUIA

Drake 1577-80

Near Santa Fé de Bogotá the ruler of an Indian tribe was anointed yearly with gold dust. From this minor incident arose the legend of El Dorado or "the gilded one." The search for this fabulous place was the mainspring of 16th century exploration of South America.

NEW GRANADA
Santa Fé de Bogotá 1538
Quito 1534
Popayán 1536
Puerto Viejo 1535
Guayaquil 1535
San Miguel 1532

U N E X P L O R E D

Orellana 1540-41
Amazon River

S O U
A M E R

U N E

P E R U

Ciudad de los Reyes (Lima) 1535
Cuzco 1535
La Paz 1548

Sucre 1540
Potosí 1546

Countries and boundaries are shown as of 1648. Dates appearing after towns, islands, etc. refer to the year of their foundation or discovery.

The name "America" was first used by the mapmaker Waldseemüller in honor of Amerigo Vespucci. At first the term referred to South America alone. Spain referred to the new world as "The Indies" or "West Indies" for centuries, however.

To the East Indies

PARAGUAY
(Jesuits 1605-1769)
Asunción 1537
Paraná River

La Serena 1544

Santa Fé 1573

COLONIAL DEPENDENCIES AND EXPLORERS' ROUTES

SPANISH
Columbus 1492
Columbus 1493-96
Columbus 1498
Columbus 1502-04
Vespucci 1497-98
Ojeda 1499
Pinzon 1499-1500
Magellan 1519-21
Orellana 1540-41
Cabrillo & Ferrelo 1542-43

PORTUGUESE
Pedro Alvarez Cabral 1500
Gaspar Corte Real 1501

ENGLISH
John Cabot 1497
John Cabot 1498
Drake 1577-80
Hudson 1610

FRENCH
Verrazano 1524
Cartier 1534
Cartier 1535

DUTCH
Hudson 1609

Magellan 1519-21

Sta. María del Buen Aire 1536
Río de la Plata

Copyright by C. S. HAMMOND & Co., N.Y.

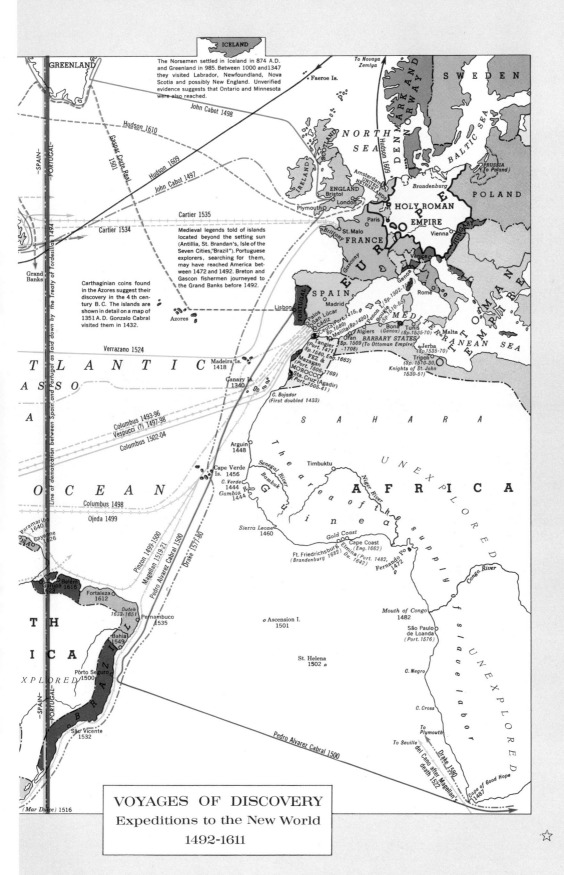

ICELAND

The Norsemen settled in Iceland in 874 A.D. and Greenland in 985. Between 1000 and 1347 they visited Labrador, Newfoundland, Nova Scotia and possibly New England. Unverified evidence suggests that Ontario and Minnesota were also reached.

GREENLAND

To Novaya Zemlya

Faeroe Is.

SWEDEN

NORTH SEA

DENMARK NORWAY

BALTIC SEA

John Cabot 1498

Hudson 1610

Gaspar Corte Real 1501

Hudson 1609

John Cabot 1497

SCOTLAND

IRELAND

Hudson 1609

PRUSSIA (To Poland)

POLAND

Amsterdam UNITED NETHERLANDS

Brandenburg

Cartier 1535

Medieval legends told of islands located beyond the setting sun (Antillia, St. Brandan's, Isle of the Seven Cities, "Brazil"). Portuguese explorers, searching for them, may have reached America between 1472 and 1492. Breton and Gascon fishermen journeyed to the Grand Banks before 1492.

ENGLAND
Bristol
London
Plymouth

HOLY ROMAN EMPIRE

Paris

Vienna

Cartier 1534

E U R O P E

Brittany St. Malo

FRANCE

Gascony

Venice

HUNGARY

Genoa

Rome

Grand Banks

Carthaginian coins found in the Azores suggest their discovery in the 4th century B.C. The islands are shown in detail on a map of 1351 A.D. Gonzalo Cabral visited them in 1432.

SPAIN

Madrid

Lisbon

PORTUGAL

Palos
San Lúcar
Cadiz
Ceuta (Port. 1415)

O T T O M A N E M P I R E

MEDITERRANEAN SEA

Menon I. (Sp. 1302-1)

Bougie (Sp. 1510-55)

Sp. 1680) Melilla (Sp. 1490)
Oran (Sp. 1509 -1708)
Algiers

Bona (Genoa) Tunis (Sp. 1535-70)

Malta

Azores

Verrazano 1524

Madeira Is. 1418

Canary Is. 1340

Tangier (Port. 1580, Eng. 1662)
FEZ & MOROCCO
Mazagan (Port. 1506-1769)
Sta. Cruz (Agadir) (Port. 1505-41)

BARBARY STATES (To Ottoman Empire)

Jerba (Sp. 1535-70)

Tripoli (Sp. 1510-30)
Knights of St. John (Sp. 1510-51)

A T L A N T I C

ASSO

A

C. Bojador (First doubled 1433)

S A H A R A

Columbus 1493-96
Vespucci (?) 1497-98
Columbus 1502-04

Arguin 1448

The Gu in e a

Senegal River

Bambuk

Timbuktu

U N E X P L O R E D

A F R I C A

Cape Verde Is. 1456
C. Verde 1444
Gambia 1444

Niger River

O C E A N

Columbus 1498

Ojeda 1499

Sierra Leone 1460

area of the supply of slave labor

Paramaribo 1640
Cayenne 1626

Gold Coast
Cape Coast (Eng. 1662)
Ft. Friedrichsburg (Brandenburg 1682)
Elmina (Port. 1482, Du. 1642)

Fernando Po 1472

Congo River

Pinzon 1499-1500

Magellan 1519-21

Pedro Alvarez Cabral 1500

Drake 1577-80

Gurupá 1623
Belem 1616
Fortaleza 1612
Dutch 1633-1661
Pernambuco 1535

Mouth of Congo 1482

São Paulo de Loanda (Port. 1576)

U N E X P L O R E D

Bahia 1549

Ascension I. 1501

St. Helena 1502

C. Negro

XPLORED

Pôrto Seguro 1500

B R A Z I L

São Vicente 1532

C. Cross

To Plymouth

To Seville

Pedro Alvarez Cabral 1500

Drake 1580

del Cano after Magellan's death 1522

Cape of Good Hope 1487

(Mar Dulce) 1516

Line of demarcation between Spain and Portugal as laid down by the Treaty of Tordesillas 1494

SPAIN PORTUGAL

VOYAGES OF DISCOVERY
Expeditions to the New World
1492-1611

for a passage to the Orient. Queen Elizabeth's swashbuckling sea dog, Sir Francis Drake, was the scourge of the oceans. He raided Spanish galleons and "singed the beard of King Philip" for England. He also sailed around South America and up the Pacific coast, where he landed in San Francisco Bay. It was Sir Francis Drake, commanding the Queen's fleet, who, aided by a great storm, defeated the Spanish Armada off English shores. After that a treaty which divided all western lands between Spain and Portugal no longer meant much.

In 1534 Jacques Cartier thrust both a cross and the white and gold banner of France into Canadian soil on the St. Lawrence River. Yet it was not until 1608 that a permanent settlement was placed beneath the high rock of Quebec. By 1608 England's Jamestown was a tiny one-year-old cluster of houses in the Virginia wilderness. One year later, in 1609, an English navigator serving the Dutch brought his little vessel, the *Half Moon*, to anchor in the harbor of the river that was to be named for him.

Captain Hudson was not the first European to see the entrance to the Hudson, for Giovanni da Verrazano had sighted it eighty-five years earlier without exploring the river. On September 2, 1609, the *Half Moon* dropped anchor in the waters of the harbor, where hills stood on one shore and a lovely green island lay on the other. Captain Hudson was excited by his belief that here he had found the fabulous waterway leading directly to the Orient. Natives paddled out in their canoes to climb aboard and stare curiously at the bearded white men. They brought gifts of feather cloaks, tobacco and corn. Henry Hudson sent an expedition up the river in a small boat to sound the depth of the water and determine whether this was the Northwest Passage. Returning to their ship these men were attacked by Indians, who sent deadly arrows into their boat, wounding several and killing the leader.

The *Half Moon* sailed a part of the way up the river, where mountains crowned the curving shores, but their captain realized that the water was growing shallower, and this was not the passageway that he sought. After a fierce fight with hostile Indians, Hudson sailed his ship back downriver past Manhattan Island, and out to sea. On his last voyage to America Henry Hudson discovered Hudson Bay. There mutinous sailors cast him ashore with his young son and a few loyal men. No one knows what happened to Henry Hudson, but, since he was employed by the Dutch East India Company, the Netherlands claimed the Hudson River and vast lands around it.

BEFORE THE WHITE CONQUEROR

On a sunny day in 1519 an Aztec village on the Gulf of Mexico drowsed among palm trees. Suddenly a native voice shouted and a hand pointed toward the water. Offshore there floated a flock of huge white-winged birds! Indians fled to the jungle to peer out at white men who were bringing strange beasts to land. A swift runner was sent to the emperor. Montezuma's palace was in his capital city set on a high plateau overlooked by snowcapped volcanoes. He called his priests and generals to council. Canoes with wings? Pale, bearded men! Could they be led by Quetzalcoatl the White God?

Quetzalcoatl was also known as the Feathered Serpent. A belief in this god had been taken over by the Aztecs from Toltecs, an earlier people of Mexico. The White God had gone away, they said, on the waters to the east, but he had promised to return bringing gifts of corn. Although white meant peace, Aztecs feared this god, for he would not tolerate human sacrifice. On the tops of pyramids Aztec altars ran with the blood of men slain by zealous priests.

Hernando Cortez, Spanish conquis-tador, landed with an army of fewer than six hundred men. He marched inland searching for gold and glory. Montezuma, in his terror, uneasily shifted his orders to the army. Sometimes they stood and fought, and sometimes they fled at sight of the horses, which they had never seen before, and at sound of gunfire.

Tenochtitlán, the capital city, was built on islands in a lake, with three causeways, connecting it to the mainland. It could have been defended well, but Montezuma allowed Cortez to enter and take him prisoner. The Aztecs, however, were not as weak as their ruler. After Spaniards had massacred a group of Indians at their temple the people rose to battle. The invaders were almost defeated escaping the city, but managed to return to the coast. There they found that ships had arrived with more men and horses. Cortez again marched on Tenochtitlán. Montezuma had been killed and Cuauhtemoc was the leader of the Aztec army. With their guns and mounts the Spaniards laid siege to the city. Cuauhtemoc, who was a man of great courage, was captured, tortured, and slain, and

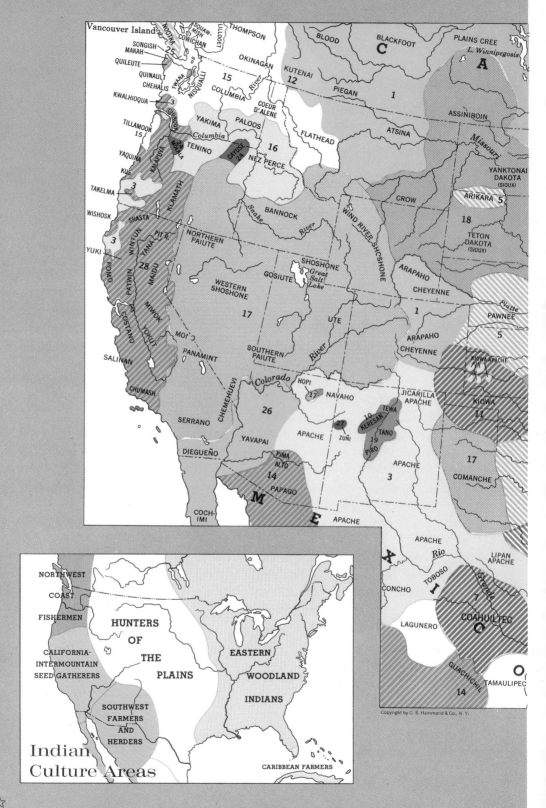

Vancouver Island

THOMPSON
BLOOD
BLACKFOOT
C
PLAINS CREE
L. Winnipegosis
A

SQUAW-MISH
COWICHAN
NOOTKA
LILLOOET
SONGISH
MAKAH
25
OKINAGAN
KUTENAI
12
PIEGAN
QUILEUTE
QUINAULT
CHEHALIS
COLUMBIA
15
River
ASSINIBOIN
KWALHIOQUA
3
NISQUALLI
COEUR
D'ALENE
ATSINA
Missouri
TILLAMOOK
15
YAKIMA
PALOOS
Columbia
FLATHEAD
YANKTONAI
DAKOTA
(SIOUX)
YAQUINA
TENINO
16
NEZ PERCE
CROW
ARIKARA 5
KUS
CAYUSE
24
18
TAKELMA
KLAMATH
SNAKE
Snake
River
TETON
DAKOTA
(SIOUX)
WISHOSK
SHASTA
NORTHERN
PAIUTE
BANNOCK
WIND RIVER SHOSHONE
YUKI
PIT R.
YANA
WINTUN
PATWIN
28
MAIDU
SHOSHONE
Great
Salt
Lake
ARAPAHO
POMO
GOSIUTE
CHEYENNE
3
WESTERN
SHOSHONE
NIWOK
YOKUT
COSTANO
17
UTE
1
ARAPAHO
CHEYENNE
Platte
PAWNEE
5
SALINAN
Moi
PANAMINT
SOUTHERN
PAIUTE
River
KIOWA APACHE
CHUMASH
CHEMEHUEVI
Colorado
HOPI
17
NAVAHO
JICARILLA
APACHE
KIOWA
11
SERRANO
26
27
KERESAN
10
TEWA
TANO
DIEGUEÑO
YAVAPAI
APACHE
ZUÑI
9
PIRO
APACHE
17
COMANCHE
PIMA
ALTO
14
PAPAGO
3
COCHI-
IMI
M
E
APACHE
APACHE
Rio
LIPAN
APACHE
CONCHO
TOBOSO
X
I
C
Rio Grande
COAHUILTEC
LAGUNERO
GUACHICHIL
O
TAMAULIPEC
14

Copyright by C. S. Hammond & Co., N. Y.

NORTHWEST
COAST
FISHERMEN

HUNTERS
OF
THE
PLAINS

EASTERN
WOODLAND
INDIANS

CALIFORNIA-
INTERMOUNTAIN
SEED GATHERERS

SOUTHWEST
FARMERS
AND
HERDERS

Indian
Culture Areas

CARIBBEAN FARMERS

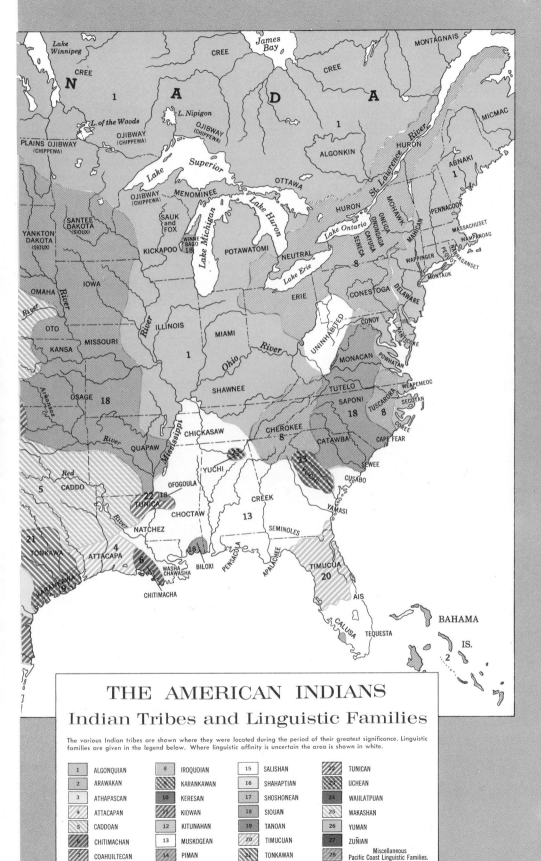

THE AMERICAN INDIANS

Indian Tribes and Linguistic Families

The various Indian tribes are shown where they were located during the period of their greatest significance. Linguistic families are given in the legend below. Where linguistic affinity is uncertain the area is shown in white.

1	ALGONQUIAN	8	IROQUOIAN	15	SALISHAN	22	TUNICAN
2	ARAWAKAN	9	KARANKAWAN	16	SHAHAPTIAN	23	UCHEAN
3	ATHAPASCAN	10	KERESAN	17	SHOSHONEAN	24	WAIILATPUAN
4	ATTACAPAN	11	KIOWAN	18	SIOUAN	25	WAKASHAN
5	CADDOAN	12	KITUNAHAN	19	TANOAN	26	YUMAN
6	CHITIMACHAN	13	MUSKOGEAN	20	TIMUCUAN	27	ZUÑIAN
7	COAHUILTECAN	14	PIMAN	21	TONKAWAN	28	Miscellaneous Pacific Coast Linguistic Families.

☆ 23

Cortez took Mexico for Spain. Cuauhtemoc the Aztec leader is a beloved hero of Mexico.

The Aztecs were the fighters of Mexico, but there had been other Indians both there and to the south before their arrival. In Yucatan and the lowlands of Central America the Mayas had already developed an advanced civilization. Their sculpture is regarded today as among the world's best. Their astronomers had an amazing knowledge of the skies, and they left a remarkable calendar cut on great stones. They invented a system of writing, and the ruins of their stone cities and temples are studied now by archaeologists.

North of Mexico Indians were less advanced in knowledge, except in the ways of nature and of tribal living. The North American continent was peopled by more than three hundred tribes of Indians. They spoke different languages and did not look much alike. In prehistoric times some lived in cliff dwellings, and then later in adobe pueblo houses several stories high. These were built on the ground, or on the tops of high rocky mesas. Indians of the dry Southwest grew corn and squash, wove baskets, made pottery, and hunted rabbits, deer, and antelope. They had religious ceremonies in underground rooms called kivas, which were entered by a ladder from a hole in the ceiling.

For a long time nomad warriors in Apache and Navajo tribes raided pueblo villages. They moved in small fighting bands, and they spoke an Athabascan language from the north. Their bows and arrows were like those used by northern forest tribes. Apaches and Navajos put up brush shelters where they camped, and did not build permanent lodges until late in the nineteenth century. Then they learned the crafts and skills of the pueblo peoples. Apaches never took to sheepherding and farm life as Navajos did until they were placed on reservations by the United States Army.

All of the tribes around the vast western plains made trips there to hunt the wandering buffalo. They came down from the Rocky Mountains to drive herds over cliffs, and then take away meat and skins on sleds pulled by dogs. Cheyenne and Arapaho, Shoshone and Ute made long journeys for the hunt. Mandans followed the buffalo and returned to their round earth lodges along the Missouri River. Blackfoot and Sioux came to the plains from the north. In California the tribes were seed gatherers, who made fine baskets for acorns and wild grain. On the northern coast along the Pacific the tribes built wooden houses, and carved totem poles. They made huge canoes to go out on the vast, unknown sea to kill the great whale.

In the far north little bands of Indians followed the herds of caribou. In winter Eskimos lived in snow igloos. They hunted seal, walrus, and polar bear. Both Indian and Eskimo had come from Asia in the unknown past, although they were of different race and language.

Woodland tribes were hunters of the deer. Around the Great Lakes and in the northeast they made their wigwams of poles covered with birchbark or the skins of animals. In birchbark canoes they paddled swiftly over lakes and on rivers. Their clothing was soft buckskin trimmed with dyed porcupine quills. Some tribes had few laws to govern them, but others were well organized both for living and for warfare. The Iroquois League of Five Nations, or tribes (later becoming six tribes) was strong and feared by all others. These Mohawks, Senecas, Cayugas, Onondagas, Oneidas and Tuscaroras lived in long houses covered with the bark of the elm tree.

Creeks, Chickasaws and Cherokees were powerful and well organized tribes in the southeast. They had many cornfields, as well as towns and villages. They made their lodges of poles roofed with leaves or bark. Some Creek settlements were called White Towns and set aside as peaceful refuges, while others were Red Towns, where warriors gathered to plan raids and warfare. With the Choctaws and Seminoles these three tribes later formed a Confederation of Five Civilized Tribes.

Along the Mississippi River enormous mounds, serpent-shaped or rounded, were left by unknown tribes. Here the "Old Ones" had worshipped or buried their dead with pottery and weapons for use in the world of spirits. The Timucuans and Calusas built such mounds, also, in Florida. These Indians were destroyed by Seminoles who broke away from their Creek tribes to move southward.

When the horse was brought to America by Spaniards, Indians on prairies and plains became remarkable riders. Horses were their most valuable possessions and pony stealing, so wrong to white men, was believed to be honorable and was much admired. The Sioux groups and other bands set up painted buckskin tepees and camped where they hunted. These wanderers of the plains belonged to tribes whose chiefs wore feathered war bonnets.

In their lodges and around campfires all Indians related tales of their gods. Gods ruled the earth, the skies, wind, rain, the sun, and the moon. Although they had sacred beliefs in the gods of nature, Indians also told odd tales of animal, bird, and fish gods who were their brothers. They spoke of their legendary hero hunters and warriors as well. Indians played rough games to condition them for battle and fun, and they developed marvelous strength and skills. They danced before they made war, or for religious ceremonies. Their way of life was based on nature, and they knew no other until the white man came.

Every European who set his booted foot on shore took a little away from the Indian. These men from the canoes that looked like great white winged birds were so few. Yet each man with a musket breathing fire and death pushed the Indian farther back — away from his ancient hunting grounds and homeland.

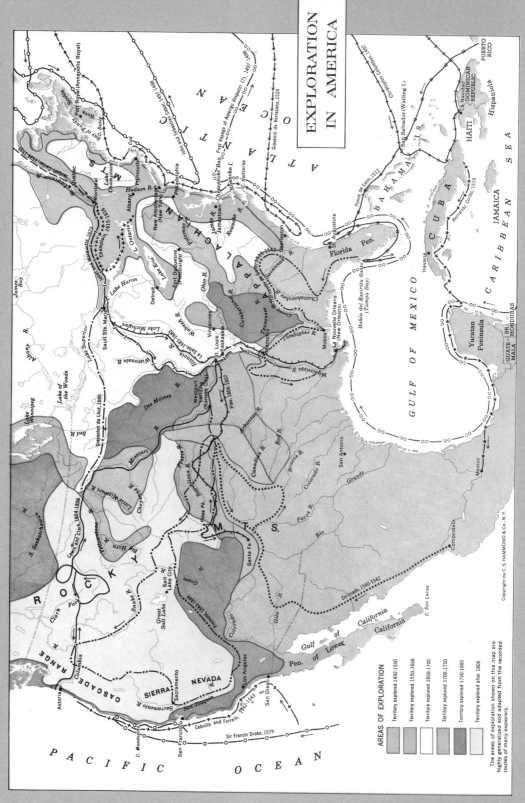

EXPLORATION IN AMERICA

CHANGING OWNERSHIP OF THE CONTINENT

English   French   Spanish   Independent

HUDSON'S BAY COMPANY

NEWFOUND-LAND

ACADIA

NEW ENGLAND

NEW FRANCE

LOUISIANA

VIRGINIA

CAROLINA

FLORIDA

NEW SPAIN

1682

NEW GRANADA

HUDSON'S BAY COMPANY

NEWFOUND-LAND

ISLE ROYALE

NOVA SCOTIA

NEW ENGLAND

NEW FRANCE

LOUISIANA

TEXAS

VIRGINIA

CAROLINA

FLORIDA

NEW SPAIN

ST. DOMINGUE

1713

NEW GRANADA

HUDSON'S BAY COMPANY

NEWFOUND LAND

QUEBEC

NOVA SCOTIA

NEW ENGLAND

LOUISIANA

VIRGINIA

CAROLINAS

TEXAS

FLORIDA

ST. DOMINGUE

NEW SPAIN

1763

NEW GRANADA

Copyright by C. S. Hammond & Co., N. Y.

HUDSON'S BAY COMPANY

NEWFOUND-LAND

QUEBEC

NOVA SCOTIA

CALIFORNIA

LOUISIANA

UNITED STATES

TEXAS

FLORIDA

ST. DOMINGUE

NEW SPAIN

1783

NEW GRANADA

THE GOLDEN DREAM

4   Although other men might venture out on stormy seas in search of treasure, Ponce de Leon was not lured to America by that dream. In a land to the west he was hoping to find a magic fountain that would bring back his youth. At the age of fifty-three this Spaniard had heard such a legend told by natives of the West Indies.

On Easter Day, six years before Cortez came as a terrible white god to the Aztecs, Ponce de Leon stepped ashore on a sandy beach near the spot where St. Augustine now stands. He called the place Florida, in honor of Easter, and claimed it for Spain. In the thick undergrowth he found a sparkling spring, but its waters did not turn his gray hair black, nor cause the wrinkles to vanish from his face. He led his men inland on a long journey on which they were attacked by Timucuan Indians in garments of gray moss, and with faces horribly painted. At last the disappointed conquistador sailed back to Cuba.

The old hunt for gold brought other men to Florida. Narváez, landing with followers and horses at Tampa Bay, made his way north and west to the "Bay of Horses," where his party had to kill their mounts for food. They tried to escape pursuing Indians by making boats and putting out to sea. A storm destroyed them, and Narváez was drowned.

Hernando de Soto's nine ships were crowded with nobles who expected to find vast riches in Florida in 1539. They landed at Tampa Bay and thrust their way through palmetto jungles northward. De Soto's men were steaming hot in heavy suits of armor, and their horses advanced slowly through the forests. Hostile Indians grew bolder in attack as they began to understand that these were not gods nor makers of magic. When de Soto reached the Mississippi he stared out over its muddy waters, discouraged by the terrible journey. He had found no cities and no riches. He had only a few men left, and they were hungry and sick. By day and night they knew that unseen eyes watched them from the dark forest. De Soto decided to try to reach Mexico, and he set his men to building boats for the voyage.

One night the little group of Spaniards gathered close around their fire.

De Soto was dead. What were they to do now? The black forest shut them in on three sides, and before them moonlight rippled on the river. The savages must not learn that the white chief had died, for that would mean an instant attack! As the moon sank low a small boat pushed silently out on the water. The body of Hernando de Soto, wrapped in a fur robe and weighted with stones, was slipped into the Mississippi River, which he had discovered. A few members of his party lived to sail out on the Gulf of Mexico, and, after a long voyage filled with hardships, some of them came safely to the Mexican shore.

While de Soto was fighting in the warm swamps and jungles of Florida, Coronado was governor of Mexico. He sat one day listening intently to a story told by a monk who had just returned from an expedition to the north. Fray Marcos spoke of the Seven Cities of Cibola, shining with golden and silver turrets and filled with piles of gems! Already Pizarro had invaded Peru, in South America, and conquered the Inca Indian empire. In a sacred ceremony the Inca emperor was covered with gold dust each year and called El Dorado, or the Golden Man. Pizarro had robbed the Incas of untold riches. Why could not he, Coronado, do the same on this continent?

He set out with three hundred nobles mounted on horses, and nearly a thousand Indians to do the work and herd the horses, cattle, sheep, and pigs. The expedition wound slowly northward, up through steep mountains, and down into valleys. After many weeks the weary would-be conquerors saw a town on the New Mexican desert. At once they prepared to lay siege to the first of the fabled seven cities. The battle was short, for this was only an adobe pueblo, defended by a few Indian warriors. Coronado was in a towering rage as he strode through the dusty streets lined with mud-brick houses. Then he moved on across Arizona, still searching for the Seven Cities of Cibola. Coronado and his party were the first white men to gaze in silent awe at the steep, red cliffs of the Grand Canyon of the Colorado.

The following summer they marched eastward, led on by a fanciful tale of a rich city told by a captive Indian. All that they found on the Kansas prairie was a cluster of earth lodges of a Quivira Indian band. Coronado, dismayed by his failure, returned to Mexico.

Some sixty years later and several thousands of miles to the northwest, Samuel de Champlain brought the first permanent French settlement to Canada. Champlain was a soldier of France and a geographer who first came out to the St. Lawrence River with a trading expedition. His second voyage was to Acadia, where he spent two winters with a company in a small fort called Port Royal. In 1608 Samuel de Champlain sailed up the St. Lawrence and chose a site for the settlement called Quebec. It was at the base of a towering rock overlooking the river. At first life in the small, fortified town was hard, for men grew sick and hungry, and fell to quarrelling and fighting. Champlain was a skilled leader, however, and he rallied his men, put down mutinies, and organized exploring and furring trips into the unknown forests.

The Algonquin tribes were friendly

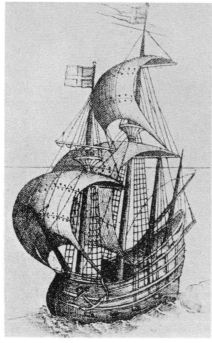
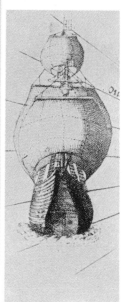

SOME OF THE VESSELS OF CHAMPLAIN AND HIS FOLLOWERS

to the French newcomers, and their chiefs held Champlain in high respect. In 1609 Champlain and two of his men joined a party made up of bands from several of these tribes, going to make war on their enemy, the Iroquois. They paddled down the Richelieu River to Lake Champlain, where Iroquois warriors were encamped. All night the three Frenchmen and Indians, in their boats, listened to the sound of a war dance on shore, for the dreaded Iroquois had seen them. At dawn the sun gleamed on the breastplates of the Frenchmen as they came in close and raised their guns. The first explosions brought down all three of the Iroquois chiefs, and the enemy fled in panic. They had never seen "devil-sticks" before. The Iroquois Five Nations never forgot this defeat, and always hated the French for it.

As his colony prospered Champlain made long journeys inland, and on one of them he discovered the Great Lakes. He also encouraged farmers to come over from France to tame the wilderness. The first French seigneur, or great landholder, was followed by others who soon came to make their system, similar to that of France, the agricultural pattern of the colony. Samuel de Champlain died just before the arrival of the first official governor, but although he never held that office he has always been known as the Father of New France.

Many other explorers went into forests and along streams also to claim these northern lands for France. Father Marquette and Louis Joliet floated down the Mississippi River in a canoe handled by Indians. They were the first explorers to see this majestic stream as far down as the mouth of the Arkansas River. Sieur de La Salle, with his friend, Tonty of the Iron Hand, explored the Mississippi to its entrance into the Gulf of Mexico.

Hot-tempered Pierre Radisson, called the Little Devil by Indian companions, set out on long trips with his brother-in-law Groseilliers, whose nickname was Gooseberries. These two were *coureurs de bois,* or runners of the woods. They traded for furs and pushed out farther into the wilderness than any other white men. In the northwest they saw musk-ox and immense herds of buffalo. They explored to the far north and returned with a scheme for a company of trading posts. When French officials would not listen they took their plan to Prince Rupert in England. This resulted in the founding of the Hudson's Bay Company. It became so strong that it did much to make England a mighty power in America.

As New France weakened, Great Britain flourished in the New World. Ownership of the continent was changing. The mighty fist of Spain loosened its hold, and New France gained no help from her mother country. English settlements came and grew and spread along Atlantic shores.

FATHER MARQUETTE

SETTLEMENTS ARE MADE

5   On a warm April day in 1607 the *Godspeed*, the *Constant*, and the *Discovery* swung at anchor off a small Virginia island. The settlers on board called their new colony Jamestown, for King James I, who had come to the English throne after the death of Queen Elizabeth. Captain John Smith was a member of the governing council for Jamestown. At once he set men to building huts for shelter on this swampy island. How well he remembered the fate of the Lost Colony twenty years before!

Sir Walter Raleigh's colony had been left by their ship on the wild coast of Virginia in 1587. That summer Virginia Dare, first white child to be born in America, had come into a dangerous world. Four years later a British expedition to the spot found no trace of the colony except a few letters carved on a tree. No one knows what happened to the colonists, or to Virginia Dare. Could it be that they were taken into a friendly tribe, or were they massacred by hostile Indians?

Captain Smith tried to persuade, and then he ordered the Virginia adventurers to work. Instead, many of them dug the ground looking for gold, and fought among themselves. When Smith was out exploring and hunting he was captured by Powhatan's Indian braves. Pocahontas, young daughter of the chief, asked that the life of this bearded white captain be spared. After that the Indians were friendly and brought game and corn to John Smith and the colony. During the second winter Ann Burras was married to John Laydon, in the first wedding on American soil. A few years later Pocahontas married John Rolfe, became a Christian, and was called the Lady Rebecca.

The Virginia London and the Plymouth Company sent colonies from England to America to establish trade, but no permanent settlements were made in New England until the Pilgrims landed there. In the town of Leyden, Holland, a few hundred Englishmen listened to strange tales, brought by sailors, of a land beyond the seas. They had left England to escape religious intolerance. America was a wilderness where no church could persecute people who refused to give up their own faith. The little separatist group of Englishmen and women had lived in the Netherlands seven years. Now they feared that their children would grow up to be Dutchmen. And so in 1620 they formed a group, calling themselves Pilgrims, and made ready to sail to the New World.

December was cold and the forest looked forbidding to the weary voyagers, as they first sighted land at the end of Cape Cod. The Pilgrims held a meeting and made a decision not to sail on to Virginia, but to find the mainland and start their colony there. They set sail again to the west and, on coming to shore, some of them went in small boats to disembark where a rock thrust up from the sand. There is a tradition that John Alden first set foot on the rock. Others claimed the same honor. But to Americans this was not important. Since 1620 Plymouth Rock has stood for the spirit and hardy strength of the Pilgrims who landed there.

Other nations were getting a foothold in the New World. Under the Dutch West India Company the colony of New Netherlands flourished quietly on the Hudson River. In the summer of 1626 Peter Minuit, first director-general, met with chiefs of the Manhattoes under a spreading tree. There the Dutch official bought from the Indians the island of Manhattan. He paid for it with goods, such as bright cloth and beads worth sixty guilders, or twenty-four dollars.

Surrounding their small log fort Dutchmen traded peaceably with the Indians, most of the time, and sent valuable furs across the ocean to Amsterdam. Each house had a garden and fruit trees, and the villagers lived comfortably, eating and drinking well.

When Peter Stuyvesant arrived as director-general he took over with a firm hand, and set up a "Rattle Watch" made up of a few men pledged to keep order by means of this first police force. Citizens in baggy breeches sat of an evening under their pear trees, puffing clouds of smoke from long-stemmed pipes. New Amsterdam might have been a pretty town in Holland.

Nevertheless, old Peter Stuyvesant had problems. It was necessary to rouse his men to fight several wars with Indians upriver, and he was also forced to attempt to oust New England settlers who moved into Dutch territory with never a "by-your-leave," and became rivals in the fur trade. Then England went to war with Holland, and British troops came to the Dutch colony. Old Peter stumped about furiously on his silver-studded wooden leg, trying, without success, to make a strong defense of the town. With a British fleet riding in the harbor, Stuyvesant surrendered on August 29, 1664, and the Dutch province became the property of the Duke of York, brother of the English King.

Swedes and Finns brought to the New World knowledge of the best way to build a log cabin. They settled on the Delaware River. William Penn found them there when he arrived with his Pennsylvania colony of Quakers in 1682. Quakers were "Plain People" who worked and worshipped quietly. Enjoying a life without arrest and persecution, such as they had not had in England, they soon made a busy town of Philadelphia. With good farms spreading out around it the "City of Brotherly Love" benefited by trade with friendly Indian tribes.

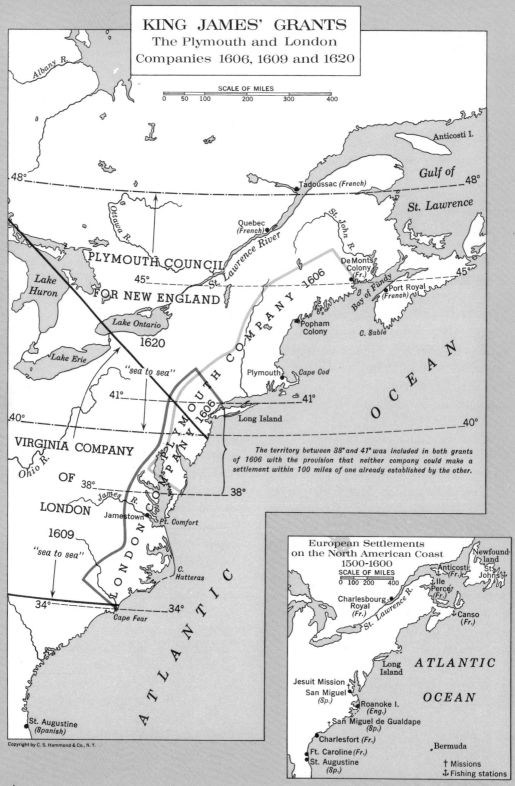

KING JAMES' GRANTS
The Plymouth and London Companies 1606, 1609 and 1620

SCALE OF MILES
0   50   100   200   300   400

Albany R.

Anticosti I.

Gulf of
48°   Tadoussac *(French)*   48°

St. Lawrence

Ottawa R.

Quebec
(French)   *St. John R.*

PLYMOUTH COUNCIL

De Monts
Colony
(Fr.)

45°   *St. Lawrence River*   *Bay of Fundy*   Port Royal   45°
(French)

FOR NEW ENGLAND

Lake
Huron

Popham
Colony

C. Sable

Lake Ontario

1620

Lake Erie

"sea to sea"

Plymouth   *Cape Cod*

41°   41°
Long Island

40°   40°

VIRGINIA COMPANY

*The territory between 38° and 41° was included in both grants
of 1606 with the provision that neither company could make a
settlement within 100 miles of one already established by the other.*

Ohio R.

OF   38°   38°

James R.

LONDON   Jamestown   *Pt. Comfort*

1609

"sea to sea"   *C.
Hatteras*

34°   34°
Cape Fear

St. Augustine
(Spanish)

Copyright by C. S. Hammond & Co., N.Y.

European Settlements
on the North American Coast
1500-1600

SCALE OF MILES
0 100 200   400

Newfound-
land

Anticosti   St.
(Fr.)   Johns

Ile
Percé
(Fr.)

Charlesbourg-
Royal
(Fr.)   *St. Lawrence R.*

Canso
(Fr.)

ATLANTIC

Long
Island

OCEAN

Jesuit Mission
San Miguel
(Sp.)

Roanoke I.
(Eng.)

San Miguel de Gualdape
(Sp.)

Charlesfort *(Fr.)*

Bermuda

Ft. Caroline *(Fr.)*

St. Augustine
(Sp.)

† Missions
⚓ Fishing stations

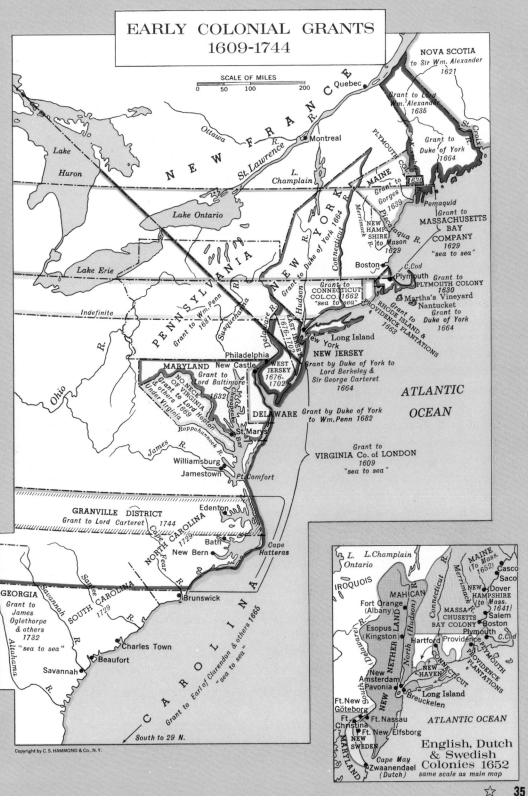

William Penn was not so friendly to Calvert, Lord Baltimore, of the Maryland colony adjoining Pennsylvania. Calvert's was a Catholic colony sandwiched between two of Protestant faith. In England both Puritans and Quakers had suffered persecution. So had Catholics under the Church of England and Oliver Cromwell's government. Lord Baltimore, like William Penn, believed firmly in freedom of religion. The Maryland colony passed an Act of Toleration, and also placed Protestants as well as Catholics on its council.

Lord Baltimore's dispute with Penn took place over the boundaries of their colonies. It was not settled in the lifetimes of either of them. A hundred years later the two colonies sent Charles Mason and Jeremiah Dixon out to survey the disputed line. They set up stones along the borders. Each fifth stone bore the coat of arms of Baltimore on one side, and of Pennsylvania on the other. Later the Mason-Dixon Line came to mean the boundary between North and South.

There were also disputes between nations over the southern colonies. Since Spain owned Florida, and England held Virginia, both claimed the two Carolinas and the Georgia area in between. The Carolina enterprise was started by a group of lords who had aided King Charles II to regain his throne. Charleston, South Carolina, was settled to be a port of trade. Its first years were defensive, and filled with scares and alarms.

"To the guns! Enemy ships coming!"

Up and down the coast Spanish raiders and pirates infested hidden coves, ready to swoop down on the town, or on English ships outward bound. The frightful cry of hostile Indian attack brought townsmen to the walls, with muskets trained on the forest fringing the backcountry. Yet each year more farms growing cotton, indigo, and rice extended out along the Cooper and Ashley Rivers. Tar and turpentine were needed by English vessels. The people who had cleared land with their own hands prospered. They built plantation mansions and brought servants over from the home country. Colonists took over the government of the Carolinas from the rule of proprietors.

James Oglethorpe sailed to Georgia with a colony of men and women who were mainly poor European farmers, and debtors from the prisons of England. There were Germans, Jews, Italians, and Scotsmen among them. Georgia as well as South Carolina suffered from Spanish raiders living in Florida. In 1740, while England was at war with Spain, General Oglethorpe marched a small army into Florida. He besieged the old stone fortress of San Marcos in St. Augustine, but failed to take it. When the war ended, Florida was deeded to England, and part of this Spanish colony was turned over to Georgia. Most of it became East Florida and West Florida.

FRENCH AND INDIAN WAR

"War! War with France!"

News came to Colonial ports in America months after the English and French had begun to fight on the high seas. Small settlements in lonely forests, on streams, and in palisaded log forts in clearings did not hear of it for a long time, if at all. Finally the struggle known as King William's War penetrated even to distant outposts.

In a freezing dawn English settlers plunged through snowdrifts to reach the fort at Schenectady. Some got through the gates before they closed, but others dropped lifeless in the snow. French soldiers and their Indian allies destroyed the fort and massacred captives. This was in February, 1690. The following month the small town of Salmon Falls, on the border of New Hampshire, was burned by a second war party sent out by Count Frontenac, governor of Quebec. A third descended on Fort Loyal, Maine, and took the outpost in a bloody battle.

Iroquois tribes had never forgotten Champlain's attack, so long before. They were always ready to make war on the French, and forts along the St. Lawrence were in danger of raids at any time. Now the Iroquois joined the British. When the French towns were attacked Frontenac retaliated. From Maine to New York English colonists were in a panic. Yet the French continued to raid and burn all along the New England frontier. Peace did not come until 1697. Even then it was only an uneasy truce for a few years.

Five years later England was fighting Queen Anne's War with France, but it was fought mainly in America, and by the colonists. A war whoop in the dawn! Shots ringing out! English settlers barricading themselves in their log cabins, shooting from windows at Indians and French troops. Isolated outposts waited, hoping for the arrival of British soldiers, but none came. Word went from one faraway fort to another, "Massacre at Deerfield. Have you heard? Sudbury — Haverhill — Wells attacked." Brutal raids left burned farms and victims of scalping. And then, at last, troops arrived from New York and Boston. The English attacked Port Royal again from the sea, and the beautiful land of Acadia fell to them. In 1713 peace was signed.

The next war lasted four years and

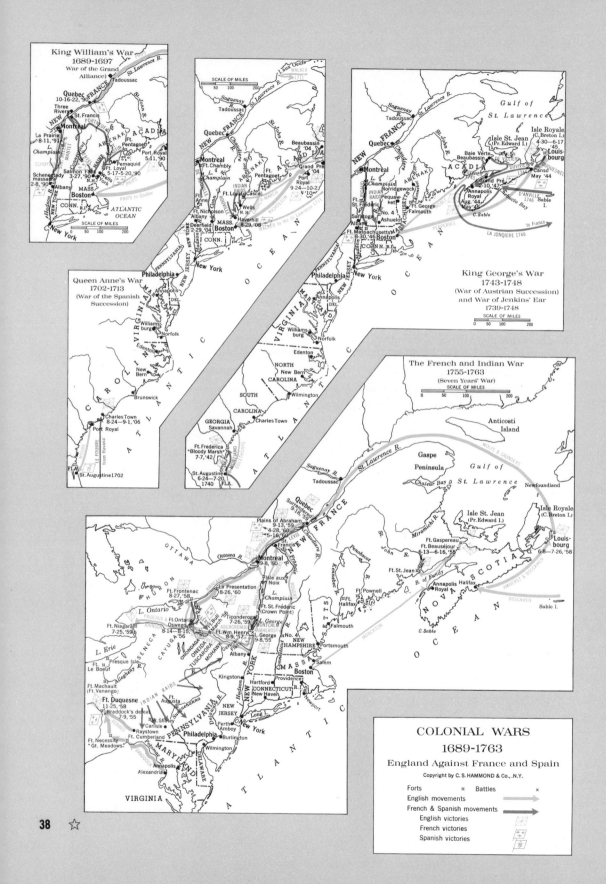

King William's War
1689-1697
War of the Grand Alliance)

St. Lawrence R.
FRANCE Tadoussac
Quebec
10-16-22, '90
Three
Rivers
St. Francis
NEW
Montreal
La Prairie
8-11, '91
L.
Champlain
St. Pentagoet
Ft. Loyal
5-17-5-20, '90
Pemaquid
Port Royal
5-11, '90
Schenectady
massacre
2-8, '90
Salmon Falls
3-27, '90
Wells
N.H.
Albany
Boston
MASS.
CONN. R.I.
ATLANTIC
OCEAN
New York
SCALE OF MILES
0   50   200

Queen Anne's War
1702-1713
(War of the Spanish
Succession)

SCALE OF MILES
50   100   200
Saguenay
R.
St. Lawrence R.
Tadoussac
Quebec
NEW FRANCE
Montreal
Ft. Chambly
L.
Champlain
Pentagoet
INDIAN
RAIDS
Ft. Loyal (Casco)
Beaubassin
'04
Grand Pre
'04
Port
Royal
9-24—10-2,
'10
Ft.
Anne
Ft. Nicholson
Albany
Deerfield
2-29, '04
Wells
N. H.
Haverhill
8-29, '08
MASS.
Boston
CONN.
New York
Philadelphia
PENNSYLVANIA
NEW JERSEY
MARYLAND
Annapolis
DEL.
VIRGINIA
Williams-
burg
Norfolk
Edenton
CAROLINA
New
Bern
Brunswick
ATLANTIC
OCEAN
Charles Town
8-24—9-1, '06
Port Royal
LE FOUBRE
from Havana
FLA.
St. Augustine 1702

King George's War
1743-1748
(War of Austrian Succession)
and War of Jenkins' Ear
1739-1748

Gulf of
St. Lawrence
Saguenay
R.
St. Lawrence R.
NEW
FRANCE
Quebec
Isle St. Jean
(Pr. Edward I.)
Isle Royale
(C. Breton I.)
4-30—6-17
'45
Louis-
bourg
Montreal
ACADIA
Baie Verte
Beaubassin
Canso
May '44
L.
Champlain
INDIAN
RAIDS
Norridgewock
Pequaw-
ket
Ft. Frederic
Saratoga
Albany
Ft. George
Falmouth
Grand Pre
'10, '47
Annapolis
Royal
Aug. '44
May '45
D'ANVILLE
1746
Sable
I.
Chebucto Bay
C. Sable
to France
LA JONQUIERE 1746
No. 4
Ashuelot
Ft. MassachusettsMASS
8-30, '46 Boston
CONN. R.I.
Philadelphia
PENNSYLVANIA
NEW JERSEY
MARYLAND
Annapolis
DEL.
New York
ATLANTIC OCEAN
VIRGINIA
Williams-
burg
Norfolk
Edenton
NORTH
CAROLINA
New Bern
SOUTH
CAROLINA
Wilmington
GEORGIA
Savannah
Charles Town
Ft. Frederica
"Bloody Marsh"
7-7, '42
St. Augustine
6-24—7-20,
1740
FLA.

SCALE OF MILES
0 50   100   200

The French and Indian War
1755-1763
(Seven Years' War)

SCALE OF MILES
0   50   100   200

Anticosti
Island
St. Lawrence R.
Gaspe
Peninsula
Gulf of
St. Lawrence
Saguenay R.
Tadoussac
Chaleur Bay
Newfoundland
Isle St. Jean
(Pr. Edward I.)
Isle Royale
(C. Breton I.)
Louis-
bourg
6-8—7-26, '58
Quebec
Surrenders
9-18, '59
Plains of Abraham
9-13, '59
4-28, '60
5-16, '60
St. Francis
NEW FRANCE
Montreal
9-8, '60.
l'Isle aux
Noix
L.
Champlain
Ft. St. Frédéric
(Crown Point)
Miramichi I.
Ft. Gaspereau
Ft. Beauséjour
6-13—6-16, '55
Ft. St. Jean
Penobscot
Kennebec
Ft. Pownell
Annapolis
Royal
Halifax
NOVA SCOTIA
Sable I.
C. Sable
OTTAWA
Ottawa R.
HUDSON
La Presentation
8-26, '60
Ft. Frontenac
8-27, '58
L. Ontario
Ft. Niagara
7-25, '59
Ft. Ontario
Oswego
8-14—8-15,
'56
Ticonderoga
7-26, '59
Ft. Wm. Henry
8-9, '57
L. George
9-8, '55
No. 4
NEW
HAMPSHIRE
Ft.
Halifax
Falmouth
Portsmouth
L. Erie
Presque Isle
Ft.
Le Boeuf
Ft. Machault
(Ft. Venango)
ONONDAGA
ONEIDA
TUSCARORA
MOHAWK
CAYUGA
SENECA
Albany
Salem
Boston
MASSACHUSETTS
Kingston
Hartford
CONNECTICUT
New Haven
Providence
R.I.
Newport
Long I.
INDIAN RAIDS
Ft. Duquesne
11-25, '58
Braddock's defeat
7-9, '55
Ft.
Augusta
Ft. Shirley
Carlisle
Ft. Necessity
"Gt. Meadows"
Raystown
Ft. Cumberland
Susquehanna R.
PENNSYLVANIA
Philadelphia
NEW
JERSEY
Perth
Amboy
Burlington
New York
MARYLAND
DELAWARE
Annapolis
Wilmington
Alexandria
VIRGINIA
ATLANTIC
OCEAN

COLONIAL WARS
1689-1763
England Against France and Spain

Copyright by C. S. HAMMOND & Co., N.Y.

Forts ⊓   Battles ×
English movements →
French & Spanish movements →
English victories
French victories
Spanish victories

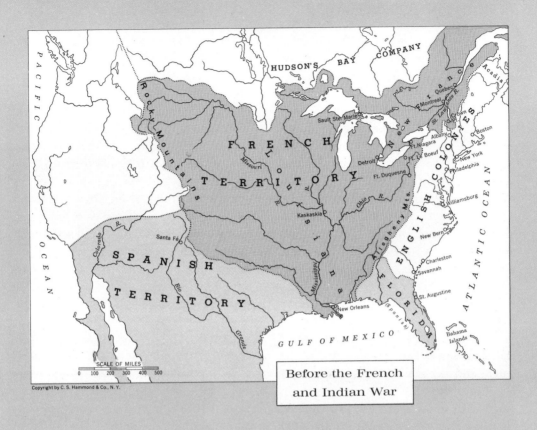

Before the French
and Indian War

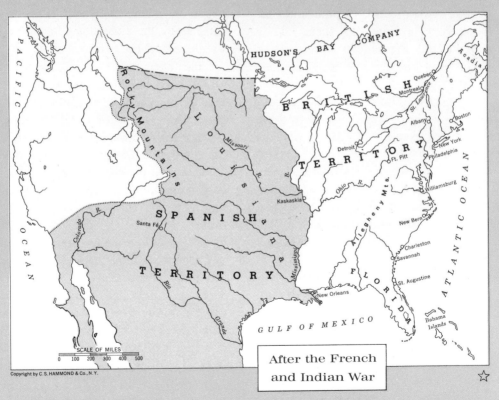

After the French
and Indian War

was caused by a severed ear. At least that was the reason given, although Englishmen knew that it was really a war for trade, and over the ownership of Georgia. Robert Jenkins was a smuggler whose ear had been cut off by Spaniards when he was caught with the goods. To arouse feeling Jenkins was brought before the British Parliament to show them his detached ear.

A few years after the War of Jenkins' Ear, Great Britain took up arms again over the ownership of Acadia, and the boundaries of New England, and the rich Ohio Valley. This time the struggle, called the French and Indian War, continued seven years, although war was not declared. It was a war of the tomahawk, the scalping knife, the torch, and the musket. Each side used the same tactics. Fighting flared up when both French and English claimed the Ohio River country. A group of fur trading gentlemen of Virginia said that the region belonged to them. They learned that Frenchmen were putting up forts as fast as they could manage to do so.

Governor Dinwiddie of Virginia sent an officer out with troops to drive the French from Fort Le Boeuf and the Monongahela River country. Lieutenant-Colonel George Washington, who had surveyed the area and knew it well, was in command. He met the French at Great Meadows, where Washington, on a previous expedition, had erected little Fort Necessity. There on "a level tract of grass and bushes," as Washington reported, the French and Indian War was begun. Both sides fought fiercely, but the larger French force had the advantage. When Washington was defeated the enemy allowed him to

march away, with his gallant men carrying their wounded.

In 1755 an English fleet sailed into Nova Scotian waters and landed on Acadia. Acadian farmers were loyal Frenchmen who had resisted British rule for a long time. In a ruthless action that separated families and friends, the British removed the Acadians to the ships and transported them to other parts of America. They were scattered along the Atlantic coast, and some were taken to the Louisiana bayou country. Longfellow wrote in poetry the sorrowful story of Evangeline, an Acadian girl, who spent her life searching for the man whom she was to marry.

In the Ohio River country warfare flared up again and again. General Braddock and his British troops were beaten by the French there, and after that defeat England sent more soldiers to defend her colonies. The victories began to swing to them. They took forts from the French, as battles were fought along the northern border.

The decisive battle of the French and Indian War took place during an assault on Quebec, on July 31, 1759. More than a month before a fleet of British ships brought redcoats up the St. Lawrence River to anchor below Quebec. Major General James Wolfe was in command of the campaign. The first attempt to take the city was a failure. With two of the English men-of-war vessels opening fire on French batteries to cover them, Wolfe's men put out for the shore in small boats. The troops rushed ashore but were caught in the fire of the French guns and forced to withdraw as a torrential downpour of rain beat them into the mud. They suffered a heavy loss of life.

Montcalm's soldiers tried to set the English ships on fire by letting the current take fire rafts down upon them, but daring English seamen caught the blazing logs and towed them ashore before they could do any damage. Above the gabled roofs of Quebec the *fleur de lis* banner fluttered defiantly on the governor's palace. In the steep streets people shrugged and smiled saying, "Englishmen cannot find a way. General Montcalm will drive them out of Canada."

And still, day after day, guns from English ships bombarded the city without destroying the strong defenses. General Wolfe planned a new attack. He sent his men out to burn and destroy the farms around Quebec, and at the same time he searched for a place where his army could climb the cliffs. General Montcalm must be taken by surprise, and attacked on the Plains of Abraham above Quebec. Weeks passed and they found no path that was not heavily guarded. Then, early in September, a renegade Frenchman told the British of a path up the cliffs from a hidden cove.

The night of the attack was dark, when a small French guard at the hidden cove was overpowered. Long lines of redcoats moved swiftly upward until General Wolfe had his army ready for attack at the top. As the sun rose it looked down on a broad field, high above the city, and on two armies facing each other. British troops stood in their red and white uniforms beside Scottish highlanders in kilts, American rangers, and Indian allies. The army of New France, making its final real stand here, was made up of regiments in the blue, white, and gold of French colonials, with wild looking woodsmen and Indian bands from several Canadian tribes.

General Montcalm's army charged the British, firing and shouting, but General Wolfe commanded his men to wait until the attackers were only a short distance away. Wolfe gave his command to fire. As Frenchmen fell back British charged. Wolfe was in the front of the battle as he received three shots in his body, and fell to the ground. An instant before he died he heard one of his men shouting that the enemy was on the run.

General Montcalm was wounded also in this battle, and was carried to his palace, where he died soon after. The surrender of Quebec, and of Montreal in the following year, gave Canada to England and ended the long rule of New France in America.

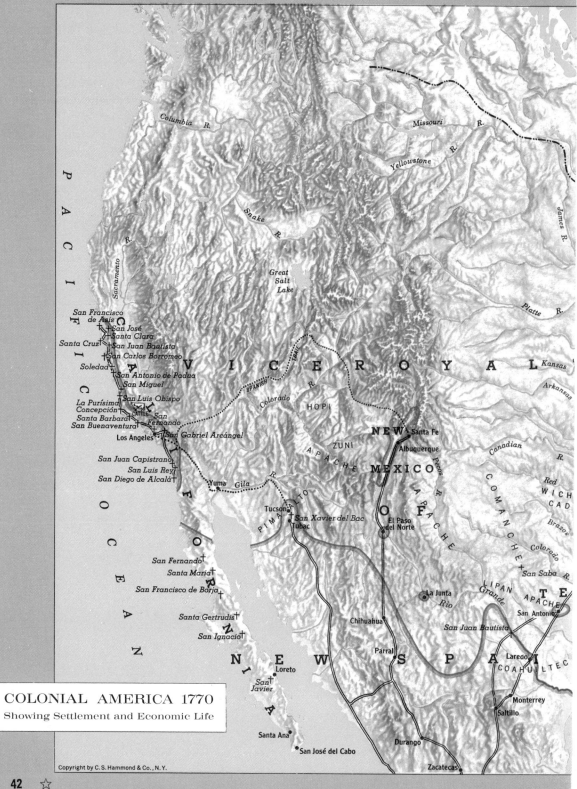

COLONIAL AMERICA 1770
Showing Settlement and Economic Life

Copyright by C.S. Hammond & Co., N.Y.

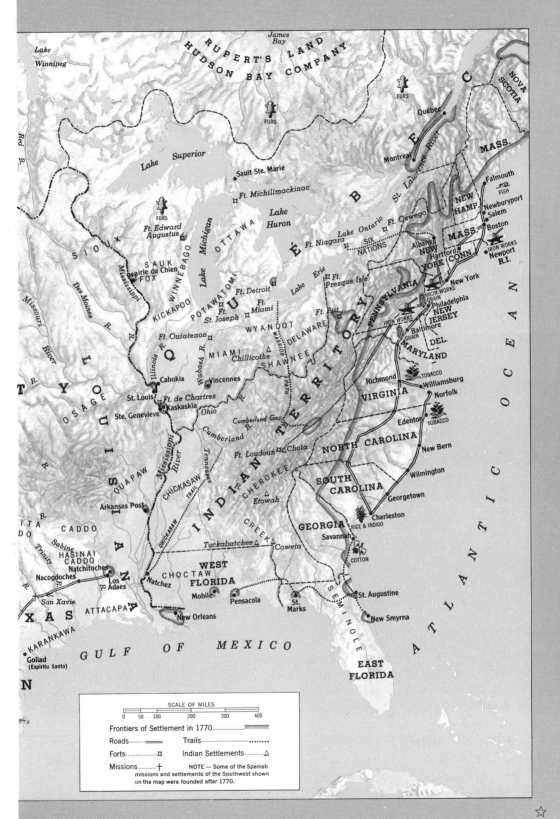

Lake
Winnipeg

Red R.

RUPERT'S LAND
HUDSON BAY COMPANY
James
Bay

FURS

Québec

NOVA
SCOTIA

MASS.

Montreal
St. Lawrence River

Falmouth
FISH

NEW
HAMP.

Newburyport
Salem
Boston
IRON WORKS
Newport
R.I.

Sault Ste. Marie

Ft. Michilimackinac

Lake Superior

FURS
Ft. Edward
Augustus

Lake Huron

Lake Michigan

OTTAWA

Ft. Oswego

Lake Ontario

Ft. Niagara
SIX
NATIONS

Albany
NEW
YORK
Hartford
CONN.

SIOUX

Mississippi

SAUK
FOX
Prairie du Chien

WINNEBAGO

KICKAPOO

POTAWATOMI

Lake Erie

Ft. Detroit

U
Ft. Miami
Ft.
St. Joseph

WYANDOT

Ft.
Presque Isle

New York
IRON WORKS
Philadelphia
NEW
JERSEY
PENNSYLVANIA
IRON WORKS
Baltimore
GRAIN
MARYLAND
DEL.

Ft. Pitt

Des Moines R.

Missouri
River

R.

Ft. Ouiatenon

Illinois R.

Wabash R.

MIAMI

Cahokia

St. Louis
Ft. de Chartres
Kaskaskia
Ste. Genevieve

Vincennes

Chillicothe

DELAWARE

SHAWNEE

WARRIOR'S PATH

Ohio

Richmond
VIRGINIA

TOBACCO

Williamsburg
Norfolk

Cumberland R.

Edenton
TOBACCO

Missouri
River

OSAGE

LOUISIANA

Cumberland Gap

NORTH CAROLINA

Ft. Loudoun
Chota

New Bern

QUAPAW

Tennessee R.

CHEROKEE

Etowah

SOUTH
CAROLINA

Wilmington

CHICKASAW TRAIL

Mississippi River

Arkansas Post

Georgetown
Charleston

CADDO

HASINAI
CADDO

Natchitoches

Nacogdoches

Los Adeas

San Xavie

TEXAS

KARANKAWA

Goliad
(Espiritu Santo)

ATTACAPA

CHICKASAW TRAIL

CREEK

Tuckabatchee
Coweta

GEORGIA

RICE & INDIGO

Savannah

COTTON

CHOCTAW

WEST
FLORIDA

Natchez

Mobile

Pensacola

St.
Marks

SEMINOLE

St. Augustine

New Smyrna

GULF   OF   MEXICO

EAST
FLORIDA

ATLANTIC   OCEAN

Sabine R.

Trinity R.

Red R.

WITA DO

ATTACAPA

New Orleans

INDIAN   TERRITORY

SCALE OF MILES
0   50 100   200   300   400

Frontiers of Settlement in 1770..............
Roads..........   Trails................
Forts..........   Indian Settlements........△
Missions..........†   NOTE — Some of the Spanish
missions and settlements of the Southwest shown
on the map were founded after 1770.

SOME WANT INDEPENDENCE

7 It was a long voyage across the Atlantic in 1770. Over in England, King George thought of his colonies as merely a source of money for his empire. In the early days colonists accepted this fact. They were busy clearing land, building farms, and working as shoemakers, silversmiths, carpenters, fishermen, trappers and traders. They had no time to think about their rights, and they took it for granted that they were part of Great Britain. But by 1770 Americans had been living in the new land a long time. The king was increasing taxes, and why should colonists stand for that?

"King George has no right to raise our taxes, and put on new ones. We can't go to Parliament to vote!"

Men were grumbling in Boston and throughout the colonies, so they spoke scornfully of the British troops as "lobsterbacks." Citizens in Boston hated to have soldiers quartered in their homes. Townsmen and soldiers insulted each other in the streets. On a chilly day in March, 1770, a small crowd threw stones at a British sentry who had knocked down a boy near the State House. As a few troops came to his aid the little mob closed in and began to fight. After their captain had been struck with a stick a British soldier fired without orders. Four men were killed and eight wounded. Bells rang an alarm, and British soldiers marched to the scene to arrest the troops who had fired. After that the British agreed to remove some of their army from Boston. Paul Revere, who was an artist as well as a silversmith, made a picture of the "Boston Massacre." This print inflamed people in the colonies against the British, even after Parliament in England had removed all the taxes imposed on the colonies except the one on tea.

The butcher, the baker, the candlestick maker! Boston was buzzing with tradesmen, artisans, and mechanics, as was every New England town and village. Families were large with ten or twelve children living in tiny houses behind shops. Hogs wallowed in the muddy or dusty streets. The harbor was a big, salty, noisy, tarry place of long wharves, ships' masts crowding in, and fishy smells. On Beacon Hill lived the satin and broadcloth, the sword and lace "codfish aristocracy," who governed the city. They owned fleets of whalers, fishing boats, and sailing vessels in and out of trading ports. They attended the Church of England on Sundays and were loyal to England until taxes became a burden. Then some of them began to think of independence, too.

Boston—New York—Philadelphia. They were different and yet alike. In all of them firewood was growing scarce and expensive. Cattle and pigs were quite at home in the unpaved streets, or on the cobbles. Epidemics of sickness and frequent fires were taken for granted. Marketplaces were crowded with produce where people met to gossip and joke as they made their purchases. Women in silk and velvet strolled about, followed by their Negro slaves or white servants, carrying home the food in baskets. Just outside of towns it was easy to hunt and fish, and in the eighteenth century anywhere in town was in walking distance for a man. Forests were close by the towns, and many slaves and white servants bound by contracts vanished into them.

On Manhattan Island New York had lost much of its quaint Dutch atmosphere by 1820. Earlier it had not been as important a port as Boston or Philadelphia, in spite of its magnificent harbor, because pirates had flourished there. Captain Kidd himself had made it his home and had openly taken part in town life. People traded in stolen pirate goods in the stores. Ships avoided New York for a long time because buccaneers lurked in nearby bays. They darted out to pursue a merchant vessel and, with the Jolly Roger flag at the masthead and a cutthroat crew

swarming over the rails, they made short work of a capture.

After some years the pirates were caught or driven away. Captain Kidd was arrested, taken to London and hanged. After that New York became a thriving port. The whole Hudson Valley prospered, with mansions of wealthy merchants rising on its highland points, overlooking the beautiful river.

Although Quakers still called themselves "Plain People," keeping to gray clothing and simple homes, they also liked good things. Their broadcloth was of the best, and so were their silver table service and fine furniture. Many families in Philadelphia were related by marriage and were making fortunes in shipping. Quaker farmers in the Pennsylvania backcountry exported grain and were doing well, too. Philadelphia was the leading city of America.

In 1774 leaders of the colonies, such as George Washington, Patrick Henry, and Samuel and John Adams, were often in the city. When General Gage brought more British troops to Boston, the First Continental Congress was held in Philadelphia to draw up resolutions and place a boycott on British goods.

South of Philadelphia along the southern seaboard proprietors of big plantations grew rich. Except for a few towns, Florida was still an unknown wilderness. In 1773 it belonged to Great Britain. Charleston, S.C., was a growing city and the busiest port south of Baltimore. Louisiana was still a Spanish possession, but the English ruled the seas.

In the mountains of the south, where deep blue valleys sheltered Creek

☆ **45**

DANIEL BOONE

and Cherokee tribes, were the backlands. These were enormous grants given wealthy colonists by the Crown. What did it matter that these were Indian lands? In 1760 Indian war burst across the backcountry. Cherokees attacked isolated forts, and burned and killed on farms, trying to drive the white men out of their hunting grounds. Troops went in to attack Indian bands. They sometimes killed women and children as well as braves, and then set fire to Indian villages.

The end of the French and Indian War in 1763 made it safer for borderers to go into the wilderness of Ohio, Indiana, and Illinois. Onward rolled the wagons, where only French traders and distant forts had been before. This was the old Northwest, land of Chief Pontiac, and to the east the country of the Iroquois. Slowly the wagons rattled along, with pioneers often finding it necessary to cut the underbrush to allow the wheels and oxen to get through. From Kentucky to Georgia long whips cracked on rough back trails. These "crackers" could send messages with whip signals from one valley to another. They drew a thin line of settlement through dense woods and along the banks of streams.

Young Daniel Boone loved the tall green trees. In 1760 he lived in North Carolina. Daniel wasn't much of a farmer, but he made a name for himself with his shooting! For many years a huge beech tree bore the inscription, "D. Boone cilled a Bar on this tree 1760"

A few years later, with one companion, he went westward into the Kentucky mountains. Along the way he met no human beings except friendly Indians. He saw enormous herds of grazing elk, deer, shaggy plains buffalo or bison. Panthers screamed in the forest trees. Wolves howled close by his camp fires. This was a wilderness where Indians did not live. The Iroquois tribes to the north and the southern Indians both called it a "place to hunt and to make war." From here the Warrior Path led north to Lake Erie. In a surprise attack Boone was captured, but he escaped from the Indians and made his way home.

In 1773 when trees spread brilliant autumn color overhead, Boone led settlers into Kentucky. They were ambushed by Shawnees and one of Daniel's sons was killed. The little group of pioneers turned back, but not until they had fought and won a battle with the attacking Indian band.

Daniel Boone founded Boonesborough in April, 1775, bringing the first permanent settlers to Kentucky. Their town, with log houses close together inside a palisade of upright stakes, was so distant that they did not learn for a long time that the American colonies were at war with England.

THE AMERICAN REVOLUTION

8

"A tax on tea? We won't pay. The *Dartmouth* is docking with a cargo of tea!"

On November 28, 1773, citizens of Boston gathered in a warehouse to hear fiery Sam Adams speak. They were told that the governor had refused to permit the ship to sail with its cargo still on board. The people of Boston, on the other hand, refused to allow the tea to be brought into the city, because they felt that they should not have to pay the tax placed on its sale.

On December 16th, the Sons of Liberty gathered, dressed themselves in blankets, feathers, and war paint, and marched to the pier.

"Boston harbor a teapot this night!"

A great crowd of citizens watched as the "Indians" climbed over the ship's rail and threw the contents of 342 boxes of tea into the water. Before the Boston Tea Party, there had been several other such demonstrations in the English colonies including one in New York harbor, but this time the colonists were infuriated. Patriots were moved to active resistance in other towns. Feeling against the mother country had not grown quickly. Eng-

lishmen had lived in America for a hundred years. Now they no longer wanted to work hard to enrich Great Britain and King George.

April — 1775! Secret activity buzzed in many places as well as in Boston. Minutemen were drilling quietly outside of town and British General Gage learned that arms were stored at Concord. In Boston a silversmith named Paul Revere, a member of the Sons of Liberty, heard that British troops were being sent to Concord. Paul Revere, who had already attended the First Continental Congress in Philadelphia, was on guard to warn of danger. He kept his eyes on the steeple of Christ Church. One lantern if by land! Two if by sea! Two lights shone out! Mounting his horse, he pounded furiously through the countryside, awakening sleeping patriots to duty.

Next day on Lexington common a line of minutemen stood with muskets aimed at trained British troops. Redcoats fired! The first shots of the American Revolution had sounded. British soldiers advanced on a small bridge at Concord, where minutemen waited. Muskets sent a charge into their ranks, and after a sharp fight, King George's men retreated. Word of the battle spread throughout the colonies.

In 1775 excitement ran through the colonies after two more events. One of them was an assault on Fort Ticonderoga, which was a partly ruined British outpost on Lake Champlain. Ethan Allen, who was a giant of a man and a brave and daring leader, gathered his Green Mountain Boys to take the fort. With fifty militiamen and Colonel Benedict Arnold added to his force, Ethan Allen started for the lake.

A big scow and two rowboats were found to carry the party to the other side, and a scout returned from a foray to report that he had located a breach in the wall. Fifty British troops were asleep at Ticonderoga when the Green Mountain Boys crept into the fort. The surprised garrison surrendered without bloodshed, and the Continental army was later able to remove and transport the big guns from Lake Champlain to Boston for General Washington to use against the British.

That same year saw the Battle of Bunker Hill which was won by the British. Yet, because Colonial militiamen had inflicted so many more casualties on their enemy than they had received from trained British soldiers, this battle seemed more a victory than a defeat to the colonists. On July 4, 1776, the Declaration of Independence was adopted by the Continental Congress, and George Washington became commander of the Colonial army. Under Lord Howe's command an English fleet arrived in New York harbor. The Battle of Long Island was a defeat for the Colonials — and yet not entirely. During the night, expert Marble-head fishermen brought Washington's army so quietly across to Manhattan Island in their small boats that even the British applauded the skill and daring of these fighting Colonials. Pulling back across Manhattan, Washington's forces fought bravely at Harlem Heights and White Plains. Then the army made a last stand on the island at Washington Heights.

Across the Hudson River, on the New Jersey palisades, General Washington watched his small rear guard lose the fort, but as they retreated the fishermen once more brought them safely over a river. The Continental army, weary and hungry, moved slowly across New Jersey to the far side of the Delaware River, fighting rearguard battles as they retreated.

When General Burgoyne brought his troops down from Canada the war took over the Hudson River Valley. This British general hoped to bottle up the American forces between his troops and the fleet. Instead, Burgoyne's army, which included Iroquois Indian allies, was badly beaten at the Battle of Saratoga.

Cold gripped the land and the Delaware River was choked with floating ice in 1776. Sleet fell in a freezing drizzle. Inside snug houses in both Trenton and Bordentown, New Jersey, Hessian soldiers, in the pay of England, ate and drank to celebrate Christmas. Feet to blazing logs, they drank toasts to their German homeland. Strange sounds out on the Delaware River were lost in the blowing wind. Why should they suspect that New England seamen were again bringing troops across a treacherous river?

Wrapped to the ears in his great-

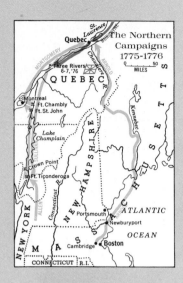

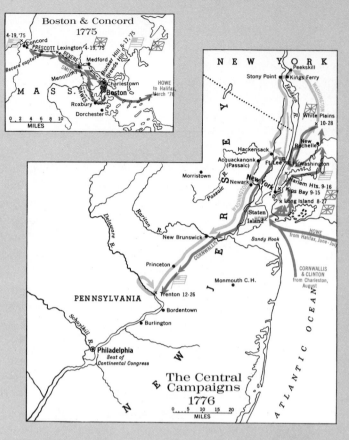

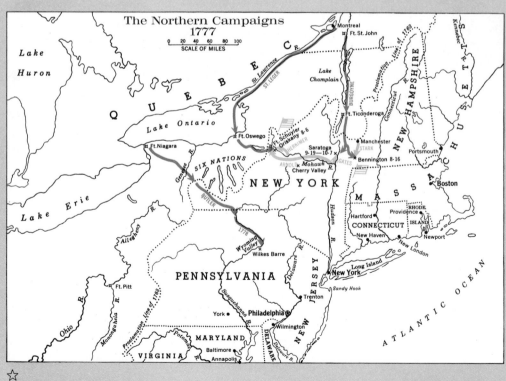

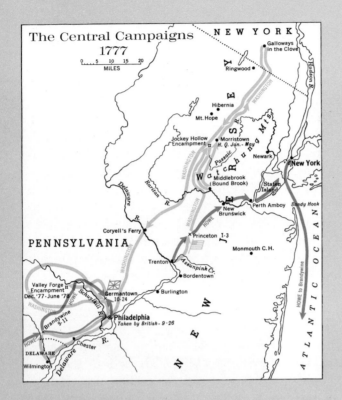

The Central Campaigns
1777

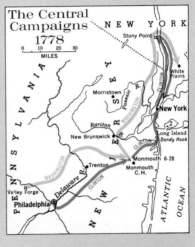

The Central
Campaigns
1778

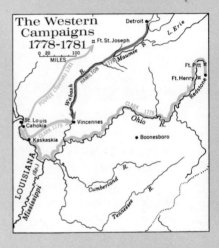

The Western
Campaigns
1778-1781

The Southern Campaigns
1780-1781

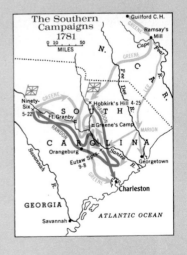

The Southern
Campaigns
1781

☆ **51**

coat, General Washington directed the surprise attack. The passage through ice-blocked water was so slow that the two columns of his army, one heading for Trenton and the other for Bordentown, could not land on the New Jersey side of the Delaware River before morning. As Washington's men crept quietly into Trenton a pale sunshine glittered on the snow. Without opposition, they placed artillery to command the streets. Hessian troops were sleeping off their Christmas party. A bombardment brought the German soldiers into the streets in wild confusion. Americans hid behind trees or fired from houses and cellars. They shot Hessians as if they were taking game in a meadow, and the British commander was killed in the battle. In Trenton, General Washington achieved a victory that lifted the spirits of the colonies and persuaded Congress to give more aid to the Continental army.

Yet the war was not won! From the sea the British took Philadelphia. Washington's army spent a terrible winter at Valley Forge, Pennsylvania. The General felt desperately anxious as he saw his ragged men, who were ill and hungry, hobbling through the snow on frozen feet. But good things happened, too. General von Steuben came from Germany to train American troops. The Marquis de Lafayette brought help from France. A Polish count named Kosciuszko designed and built a strong fort at West Point on the Hudson River to hold back the British. Colonial soldiers were still hanging onto the Hudson Valley, even after defeats in New Jersey. In spite of their losses American spirits began to rise, and hope filled their hearts.

Fighting moved into the south, with the British General Henry Clinton occupying Savannah and Charleston, then later withdrawing to the north again. In the autumn of 1780 a British major took a thousand Loyalist volunteers with some British regulars on a raid into western South Carolina. Grim frontiersmen gathered until a force of two thousand expert mountain men were in hot pursuit of the British. They caught them taking refuge on King's Mountain. There the English made a stand at the top, from time to time charging with bayonets on frontiersmen who crept up the mountain on all sides. These American marksmen, however, only slipped back into the trees and shot British soldiers from cover. At the end of this bloody battle the British commander fell and his men ran up a white flag. A large supply of arms was taken. Sir Henry Clinton commanding the British forces said that the Battle of King's Mountain was the first link in a chain of events that ended in Britain's final loss of America. It was the turning point of the war. A French fleet soon sailed in to aid the Colonists in the fighting along the Virginia coast.

At Yorktown, British General Cornwallis surrendered to the Continental army. Mighty England had been defeated in a six-year war with "a handful of Colonials armed with squirrel guns." The United States of America became a fact when the peace treaty was signed nearly two years later.

A NEW NATION

Bowery Lane in New York was thronged. Cheering, shouting citizens jostled against venders who were crying, "Hot corn! Sweet potatoes!" Children ran and sang and dogs barked in an air charged with excitement.

"There he comes! It's George Washington!"

Sound of drums rolling, marching feet, and into view came the general's tall figure seated like a statue on his horse. Behind him his army stepped proudly. This was Evacuation Day — November 25, 1783, and the British had gone. General Washington said farewell to his army, and then to his officers at Fraunces Tavern. His work accomplished, he went home to Mount Vernon on the Potomac.

Not long afterward Washington returned as the first president-elect. His inauguration took place in New York, the temporary capital, on a soft April day in 1789. He stood on a balcony at Federal Hall. The new flag with its thirteen stars whipped in a salty breeze from the harbor. Packed streets echoed with cheers as Robert Livingston shouted, "Long live George Washington! President of the United States!"

The capital was soon moved to Philadelphia. It remained there from 1790 to 1800. In historic Independence Hall the Declaration of Independence and the Constitution had been approved. Today, the cracked Liberty Bell stands in its rotunda. It is inscribed, "Proclaim Liberty throughout all the land unto all the inhabitants thereof."

As he pursued his task of establishing the United States, the president also planned the new capital city of Washington. His architect was L'Enfant, a Frenchman who had been with the Colonial army at Valley Forge.

George Washington believed in a strong central government. The first Congress appointed a committee to draft amendments to the Constitution which would protect the rights of individuals from any infringement by the government. Ten such amendments were ratified by the states. They became known as our Bill of Rights. However, the Constitution was no sooner adopted than members of Congress divided into two groups. Some, like the President, believed in a strong central government. Others wanted the

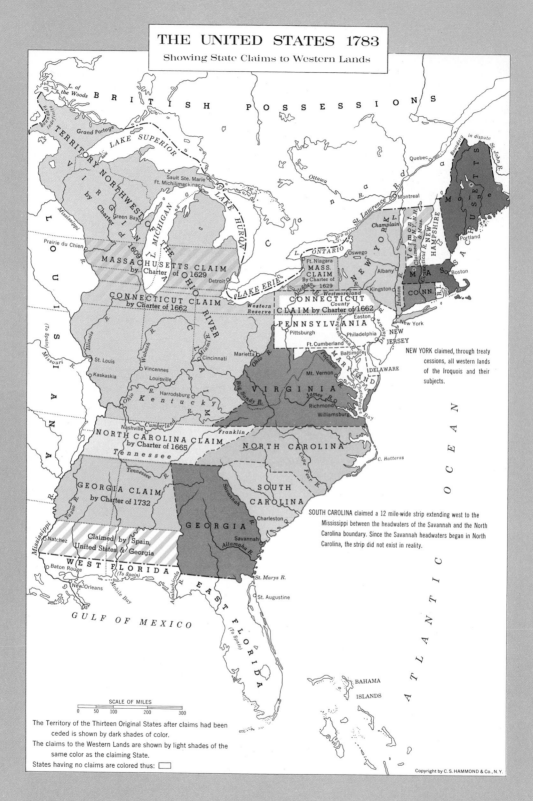

THE UNITED STATES 1783
Showing State Claims to Western Lands

NEW YORK claimed, through treaty cessions, all western lands of the Iroquois and their subjects.

SOUTH CAROLINA claimed a 12 mile-wide strip extending west to the Mississippi between the headwaters of the Savannah and the North Carolina boundary. Since the Savannah headwaters began in North Carolina, the strip did not exist in reality.

The Territory of the Thirteen Original States after claims had been ceded is shown by dark shades of color.
The claims to the Western Lands are shown by light shades of the same color as the claiming State.
States having no claims are colored thus:

SCALE OF MILES
0   50   100   200   300

Copyright by C. S. HAMMOND & Co., N.Y.

54 ☆

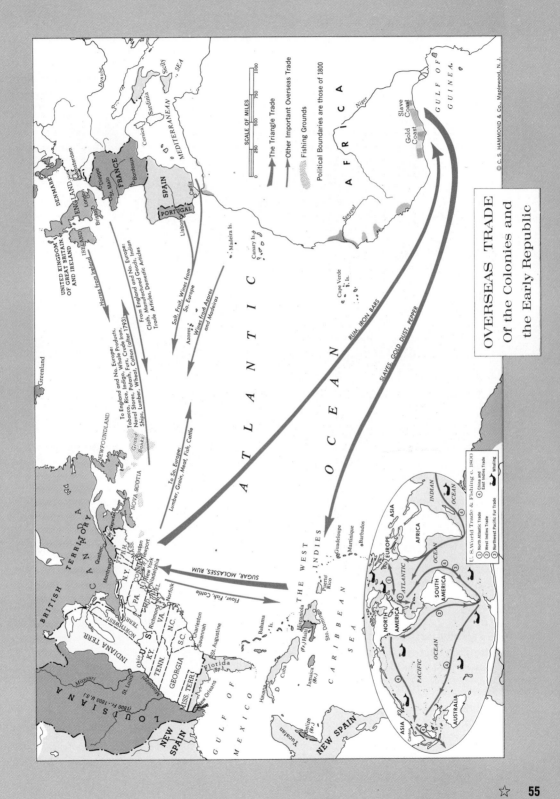

OVERSEAS TRADE
Of the Colonies and
the Early Republic

SCALE OF MILES

The Triangle Trade

Other Important Overseas Trade

Fishing Grounds

Political Boundaries are those of 1800

© C. S. HAMMOND & Co., Maplewood, N.J.

U. S. World Trade & Fishing c. 1800

① North Atlantic Trade
② West Indies Trade
③ Northwest Pacific Fur Trade
④ China and East Indies Trade
Whaling

To England and No. Europe:
Tobacco, Rice, Indigo, Furs, Crude Iron,
Naval Stores, Potash, Wheat, Cotton (after 1793)
Ships, Lumber, Domestic Articles

From England and No. Europe:
Cloth, Manufactured Goods, Indian
Trade Articles, Domestic Articles

Whale Products:
To England and No. Europe:

Horses from Ireland

Salt, Fruit, Wines from
So. Europe

Wines from Azores
and Madeiras

To So. Europe:
Lumber, Grain, Meat, Fish, Cattle

SUGAR, MOLASSES, RUM

Flour, Fish, Cattle

SLAVES, GOLD, DUST, PEPPER

RUM, IRON BARS

states to have more independent rights. Was Congress to hold to a strict interpretation of the Constitution? How much power should the Supreme Court have? Over the years this became a political issue—and it is still one today.

The Bill of Rights established religious freedom, freedom of the press and of speech, the right of peaceable assembly, and the right to petition the government for a redress of grievances. No person should be tried twice for the same crime, or be a witness against himself. He could not be deprived of life, liberty, or property without due process of law. These were some of the basic rights laid down for our citizens in our democratic form of government.

As the Revolution ended the thirteen states settled into a democracy such as the world had not seen before. Americans felt independent. They were strong and active, curious, and eager. Many were moving into wilderness lands beyond the Appalachian Mountains. Others drifted along on rafts down swift flowing rivers. The states made claims to these Indians lands. They wanted pioneers to push out and draw new country into the nation.

The Great Lakes hung down like a giant bunch of grapes from the Canadian border into old Northwest Territory. Michigan — Indiana — Illinois — Wisconsin — these lands were claimed by Massachusetts, Virginia, and Connecticut. But Congress was given authority over the region. Ordinances were set up to provide rules for its government; surveys and land divisions were made. There was just one obstacle. Although France had ceded it to England, Indians believed that they owned this country! Congress could not easily remove the Indians from America.

There were few settlers in that wide land of forests, prairies, and rivers. For some time fierce Indian resistance kept white men to the Ohio River Valley, but after General Wayne defeated the Indians at Fallen Timbers in 1794 borderers came rolling into most of Ohio. A few years later the Ohio and Indiana Territories were formed. Although it was still wild, Ohio became a state in 1803. The new nation was stretching its boundaries.

Louisiana was enormous, extending from the Gulf of Mexico to Canada, and out to the Rocky Mountains. It was the home of Indians and mountain men. There prowled the bear, while the antelope grazed in foothills, and buffalo moved across the plains. Emperor Napoleon of France needed money in 1803, so he sold Louisiana to the United States. President Jefferson then sent Lewis and Clark to the west to bring back scientific information of the geography of that almost unknown land. This knowledge would also help put Americans into the fur trade out there.

As soon as the spring thaw had freed the rivers and greened the tops of cottonwoods along the shores, flatboats moved up the muddy Missouri. The white men were well received by Mandan and Arikara tribes in their domed earth lodges behind palisades. Lewis and Clark and their party spent the next winter with the Mandans. When spring came again they hired as a guide a Frenchman who knew some of the tribal languages. He took along his wife and baby son. She was called Sacagawea, the Bird Woman, and was a Shoshone, or Snake tribal woman. Sacagawea had been stolen and sold to another tribe in childhood. She offered to lead the party west to her own land.

The success of this long and dangerous journey was brought about largely through the Bird Woman. She found her people and made them friendly to Lewis and Clark. Then she guided the expedition safely back to the Missouri River. Trade followed, and settlements gradually were made. Now Easterners seemed to have one eye on the unexplored west, and the other on established trade by sea.

Atlantic ports were centers for foreign exchange of goods and money. Before the Revolution merchant vessels had plied the Three-Cornered Trade — from a northern port such as Boston to the Gold Coast of Africa to a port in the West Indies. And a fair wind home again! In 1752 the brigantine *Sanderson* had sailed with a cargo of New England distilled rum and iron bars forged in Pennsylvania and New Jersey. These small bars of iron were used in place of money in Africa. The vessel also carried tar and flour, as well as plenty of shackles for slaves. In Africa the cargo was exchanged for slaves, gold dust, and pepper. These were taken to the West Indies and sold. The *Sanderson* then sailed home to Newport, Rhode Island, her hold filled with sugar for rum making. She also carried bills of exchange on Liverpool, England. These were to be used for the purchase of British goods, which were denied to Americans except through English ship-ping firms, and with taxes imposed.

After the end of the War of Independence, England closed all of her ports in the West Indies to American vessels. But Yankee ship captains often found a way around that and slipped into port secretly. American sailors were known everywhere for the bravery and seamanship which had played such a large part in winning independence for the United States.

By the 19th century American whaling vessels were known throughout the world, while Nantucket and New Bedford, Massachusetts, were famous whaling ports. Their houses had little flat roofs called "captains' walks", where wives could watch for sight of sail on the horizon. In the 1840's a whaling voyage took four or five years. At this period there were more than seven hundred whaling ships out on the seas at the same time. At the cry of "Thar she blows!" small boats put out from the vessel. The harpooner stood at the bow. "Strike!" His harpoon sank in the whale, and, throwing spray high in the air the quarry raced away, pulling the boat along at a dizzy speed. When he tired the mate threw his spear, and the carcass was towed to the ship, where it was cut up and the oil boiled from the blubber. For a hundred years America led the whaling trade, until the discovery of petroleum took the trade away from whalers and ruined their market.

GUNFIRE ON THE SEAS

10 When the colonies struck for independence they had some tough vessels and many seafaring men as skillful and daring as any on salt water. But they had no navy. By Congressional order the Continental navy was started with the purchase of two old ships. Marines, more ships and a commander-in-chief were soon added. The new naval vessels attacked British merchantmen, and seized cargos. They also brought munitions from France to the struggling colonies.

On a bright September afternoon in 1779, a battered and not too seaworthy craft beat up the English coast. Commander John Paul Jones, pacing the quarterdeck of his flagship, the *Bonhomme Richard,* turned his glass on the horizon. He saw two British warships. The *Serapis* and the *Countess of Scarborough* were carrying naval stores. Commander Jones weighed his chances. His ship was old, and her forty-two guns likely to blow up. Nevertheless, the commander gave orders to maneuver the *Bonhomme Richard* alongside the *Serapis.*

"Fire!"

A broadside roared. In a burst of flame two guns on the *Richard* exploded, killing their crews. Cannon on the *Serapis* flashed and boomed. Then the American commander sent his ship directly across the enemy's bow, where bowsprit and mast tangled. John Paul Jones roared out an order to lash them together. The battle raged on both vessels, with cannonballs bursting through the hulls. The British captain shouted for surrender of the American ship.

"I have not yet begun to fight!" replied John Paul Jones.

He turned around in time to see a gunner running down the Stars and Stripes. The captain flung his pistol at the man and knocked him to the deck. The American flag flew high. Darkness fell, with the battle still swaying back and forth. The *Richard* was leaking badly, so her commander put his British prisoners to the pumps. Suddenly a seaman from the *Richard* darted across the locked yardarms and tossed a grenade into the open hatch of the enemy ship. An ammunition store exploded with a deafening blast. The *Richard's* cannon followed, taking off the mainmast of the *Serapis.* Cap-

From a painting by Thomas Birch

FRIGATE "CONSTITUTION" ENGAGING THE "GUERRIÈRE"

tain Pearson lowered the Union Jack and surrendered to John Paul Jones.

In the year 1801 American ships were being boarded and robbed by pirates sailing out of North African ports. There had always been sea robbers in the Barbary states, and their governments were run on pirate loot taken from ships of all nations. Other countries had fought Barbary pirates for hundreds of years, and never with much success. America was outraged when her seamen were captured and flung into North African dungeons. Americans shouted, "No more blackmail to Barbary pirates!" A squadron of four fighting ships was sent out under Commander Dale.

During a blockade of Tripoli by American ships in 1803 the frigate *Philadelphia* sailed too close to a hidden reef while chasing a pirate craft. Unable to float off, she was capturd by enemy ships and her crew was put in prison. Then the Tripolitanians refloated their American naval prize.

The night of February 16, 1804 was as black as a Barbary coast dungeon. Only the sloshing of waves against the hull of the *Philadelphia* broke the silence. The dim shapes of small boats slipped alongside and men in Maltese disguise swarmed over the rails. They jumped the Tripolitanian crew and threw them overboard. Lieutenant Stephen Decatur with his eighty volunteers cleared the ship and set her on fire. In a daring move they escaped to their ship, the *Intrepid,* and took her out of the enemy harbor like a phantom, with all hands working at the oars.

America laughed in delight at Decatur's exploit. The Barbary pirates were not cleared away for some years, yet now sea robbers were not so bold, and the seas were safer for American ships.

When America went to war with Great Britain again in 1812 many battles were fought on the seas. Some were between old friends, sea dogs, who had been in the British navy together. Now with hostilities declared, they were enemies. Captain Hull, of the United States *Constitution,* known as *Old Ironsides,* had long been a friend of Captain Dacres of the British *Guerrière.* After war broke out these two captains were out looking for each other. They had bet their hats on a duel between their ships.

With the war only two months old the *Constitution* sighted the *Guerrière* off Nova Scotia. Hull bore down on the enemy ship, drums rolling on deck, and the battle was joined. The *Constitution* had fifty-two guns and the *Guerrière* fifty. As they pounded each other Captain Hull rushed about so violently that his breeches split. This did not slow him up, however. The fight lasted until the masts of the British ship came down. Captain Dacres, who was wounded, offered his sword in surrender, but Hull refused it. As the American commander helped his old friend over to the *Constitution* he barked out, "And now I'll trouble you for your hat, sir!"

The poem, "Old Ironsides," was written by Oliver Wendell Holmes. It is believed that a seaman who saw shot denting, but not breaking, her oaken hull gave her the beloved name.

In 1812, while England and France were at war with each other, British ships captured American vessels and put the crews in prison. This might have been settled by arbitration between the governments had it not been for the war hawks. These were hot-blooded young congressmen who were mainly from the South and West. They wanted war with England.

Great Britain resented American privateersmen — those fighting seamen who went out in their strong old ships to prey on English shipping. During the war of 1812, while American warships had the main task of fighting the British navy, American privateers captured English merchantmen. These privateers, sailing under high masts, were fast and stripped for action. Beautiful to see under their billowy sails, they were both raiders and blockade runners. They slipped away and laughed at the British, who tried to bottle them up in ports.

The War of 1812 brought battles on fresh water, too. On the Great Lakes Oliver Hazard Perry, fleet commander, sailed in his flagship, the *Lawrence*. It had been named for Captain Lawrence, who was killed in a sea fight with the British outside of Boston harbor. As Lawrence lay dying on deck he gasped, "Don't give up the ship!" Perry's flagship flew a blue flag with his friend's last words on it.

After Commander Oliver Hazard Perry won the Battle of Lake Erie he sent a famous message to American Major General W. H. Harrison at the Canadian border. It read: "Dear Genrl: We have met the enemy, and they are ours, two ships, two brigs, one schooner and one sloop. Yours with great respect and esteem. O. H. Perry."

With peace times in the 1800's fortunes were made in the China trade. Ships used as privateers in the war with England in 1812 went into trading. In China only one port was open to foreigners for a long time. This was Canton, where American ships, with their bright sails, came into the harbor among hundreds of Chinese sampans and junks. They joined vessels from all over the world at anchorage there. Western ships carried all sorts of goods, including tools and music boxes, to trade for delicate plates, cups, and fragrant tea. Shipping merchants became rich in all of the Atlantic ports from Maine to Georgia.

The clipper ship was the most beautiful of all vessels. She was sharp in line, and fast, with tall masts carrying sails that made her look like a great bird poised on the waves. Some of the famous clippers were built in Baltimore shipyards. They sailed around Cape Horn to the Orient, and also carried men to the wild gold fields of California in 1849. Their sailors were called "iron men in wooden ships," and famous tales have been written about them. Men trained on clipper ships were hardy and brave enough to challenge the might of Great Britain on the seas in the War of 1812.

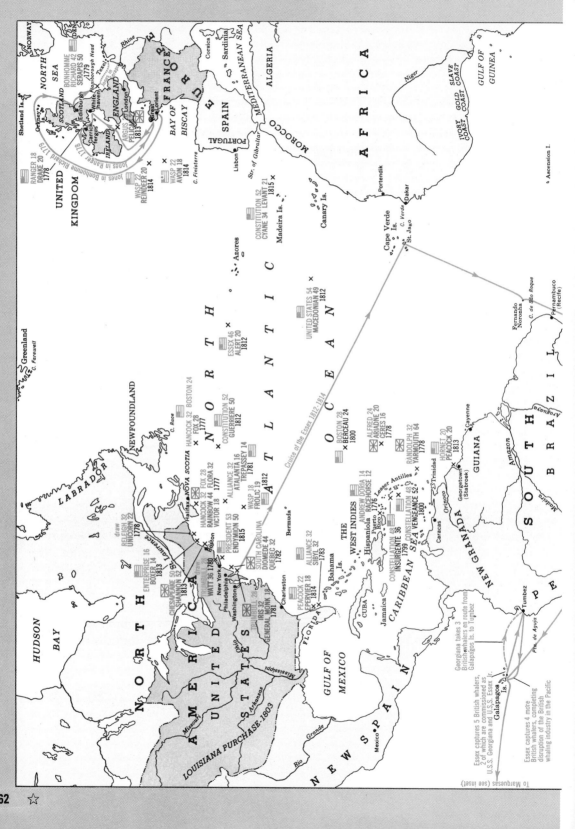

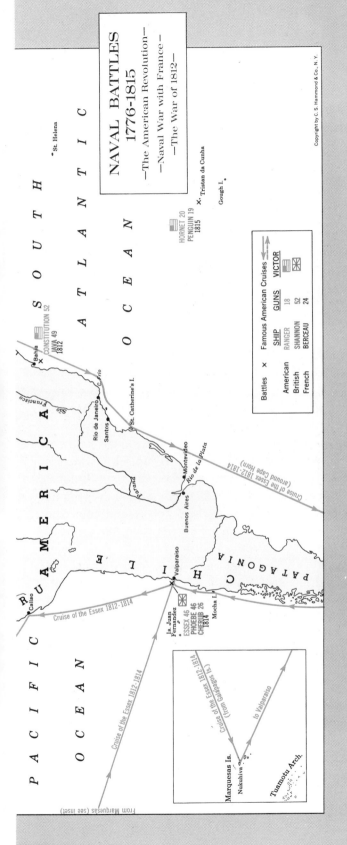

NAVAL BATTLES
1776-1815
—The American Revolution—
—Naval War with France—
—The War of 1812—

Copyright by C. S. Hammond & Co., N. Y.

Famous American Cruises

SHIP	GUNS
RANGER	18
SHANNON	52
BERCEAU	24

Battles ×

VICTOR

American
British
French

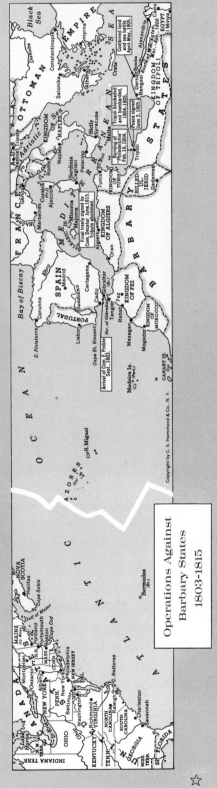

Copyright by C. S. Hammond & Co., N. Y.

Operations Against Barbary States
1803-1815

☆ **63**

WE FIGHT THE BRITISH AGAIN

11 War hawks in Congress called for exploits on the land as well as on the seas. "Take Florida! Canada must be ours!" At the same time, in the old Northwest Territory, a great Shawnee military leader, Chief Tecumseh, was organizing a confederation of tribes to drive out encroaching Yankees. He had earlier been defeated by the American General Harrison at Tippecanoe. Now he joined the British forces.

War with Great Britain in 1812 found the United States unprepared and badly unorganized on land. It was difficult to get men to enlist in this war, and when they were finally brought into the army they had to be trained. Some of the states were opposed to the war and refused to cooperate. Yet President Madison and his advisers ignored all of these factors, and called for an invasion of Canada.

The beginning of the campaign in the north was a series of defeats for American troops at Detroit, Fort Dearborn (where Chicago was later founded), and on the island of Michilimackinac. The Battle of Niagara was won by Canadians under General Isaac Brock, their most able commander, who was killed in this encounter. While the campaigns of the next two years in the north were slowly turning in favor of the United States, important sea battles were won on the lakes.

General Harrison pursued the English and their Indian allies across the border to the Thames River in Canada. An exhausted British regiment held the left flank, while Tecumseh's warriors stood their ground on the right. Colonel Johnson's United States regiment charged on their horses and took the British line. The Shawnee warriors still held out, fighting bravely, until Chief Tecumseh fell. Then they disappeared swiftly and silently into the forest, taking the body of their chief with them. This ended the uprising of united Indian tribes, and it gave control of the old Northwest to white settlers and the United States government.

If the old Northwest was safer in 1814 — not as much could be said for the capital city of the land. The United States Congress had shouted for war, and made few preparations for it! The defense of Washington had not even been planned. On a hot and dusty August day British troops, led by General Ross, marched against the capital city. American men rushed bravely to the defense, but they were untrained and they faced the expert British army. Five thousand militiamen stood ready to hold the city. At sight of the solid ranks of redcoats, and with cannon belching fire and ball, the volunteers fled in panic. But there was one man who did not run. Commodore Joshua Barney, with a small force of sailors and marines, turned a withering fire on the enemy. He did not give up until his few hundred defenders were nearly destroyed and he was badly wounded.

The August sun was on the American side. British troops, with no opposition against them, could not advance. They fell down with sunstroke, and were forced to wait until after sundown to march into the almost deserted city of Washington.

President Madison rode furiously with the retreating volunteer army, trying to rally them to the defense. Two days earlier he had urged his First Lady, Dolley Madison, to leave Washington. She waved good-bye to the President as he galloped away, and then she went into the White House to pack important cabinet papers in a trunk. From time to time she climbed to the roof to peer through a spyglass at the road that the British might take. Madison sent a note to Dolley by a fast messenger, telling her to have a carriage ready to leave at an instant's notice. She ordered a carriage, and put into it valuable government papers, along with the White House silver service.

The mansion was almost as deserted as the city. A guard and the servants, left for Dolley, had disappeared. She was alone with one servant, French John, who offered to set up a cannon at the gate and blow up the first British detachment who came. This she refused to let him do. Wild rumors flew about the ears of the First Lady as a few friends came and went. Somebody had poisoned the President! Spies dressed as women were planning to steal the state papers? Dolley Madison did not believe any of them. In the distance guns roared and shook the White House windows. Dolley spent most of her time on the roof as the battle was lost. Friends rushed over again to beg her to leave with them. She secured a wagon and packed it with White House valuables. Once, even in her hurry, she paused before a painting of George Washington. How could she leave that to British vandals? Since the frame was too big to transport she asked friends to break it up. Then she took the canvas with her.

Jumping into the carriage Dolley Madison, followed by her wagon, rolled swiftly out of the desolate city. President James Madison, his horse covered with foam, arrived to find her gone and he took off in pursuit. Down in Virginia he caught up with her at a little wayside inn. That night British troops entered the capital to plunder and burn it. Citizens with faces set in grief and fury watched from a distance as the White House, the Capitol, and other buildings went up in flames.

Off Fort McHenry, in Chesapeake Bay, British guns flashed in an attempt to take Baltimore. All night long the cannonade continued. An anxious man, standing on the deck of a British warship, peered into the darkness. Would the fort fall — or would it hold? He was an American who had come out

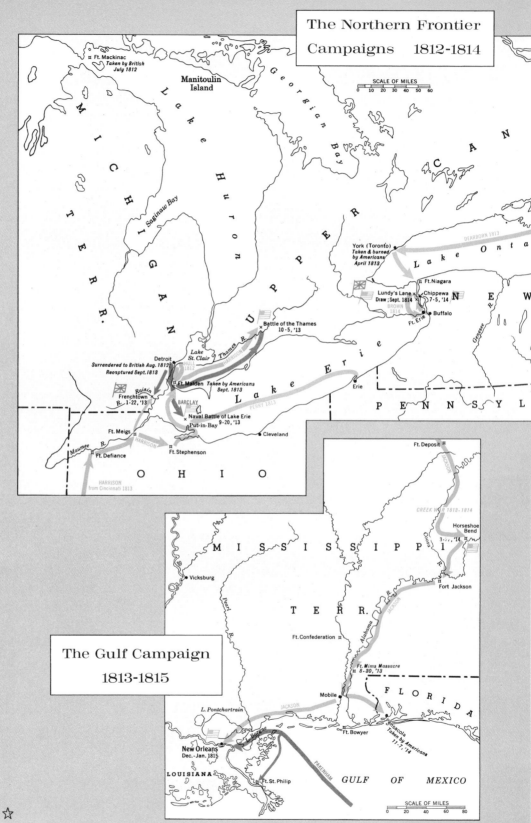

The Northern Frontier
Campaigns   1812-1814

Ft. Mackinac
*Taken by British
July 1812*

Manitoulin
Island

Georgian Bay

SCALE OF MILES
0 10 20 30 40 50 60

U P P E R   C A N

M I C H I G A N   T E R R.

Lake Huron

Saginaw Bay

York (Toronto)
*Taken & burned
by Americans
April 1813*

Lake Onta

DEARBORN 1813

Ft. Niagara
Lundy's Lane
Draw ; Sept. 1814
Chippewa
7-5, '14

N   E   W

BROWN
1813

Buffalo

Battle of the Thames
10-5, '13

Ft. Erie

THAMES 1813

Thames R.

Lake
St. Clair

Detroit
Surrendered to British Aug. 1812
Recaptured Sept. 1813

HULL
1812

Raisin R.
Frenchtown
R. 1-22, '13

Ft. Malden *Taken by Americans
Sept. 1813*

BARCLAY

Naval Battle of Lake Erie
Put-in-Bay
9-20, '13

Lake Erie

Erie

P E N N S Y L

Ft. Meigs

HARRISON

Maumee R.

Ft. Defiance

Ft. Stephenson

Cleveland

O H I O

HARRISON
from Cincinnati 1813

Ft. Deposit

M I S S I S S I P P I

CREEK WAR 1813-1814

Horseshoe
Bend
3-??, '14

JACKSON

Coosa R.

Fort Jackson

The Gulf Campaign
1813-1815

Vicksburg

Pearl R.

T E R R.

Ft. Confederation

Alabama R.

JACKSON

Ft. Mims Massacre
8-30, '13

F L O R I D A

Mobile

L. Pontchartrain

JACKSON

Ft. Bowyer

Pensacola
*Taken by Americans
11-7, '14*

New Orleans
Dec.-Jan. 1815

L. Borgne

Ft. St. Philip

PAKENHAM

G U L F   O F   M E X I C O

L O U I S I A N A

SCALE OF MILES
0   20   40   60   80

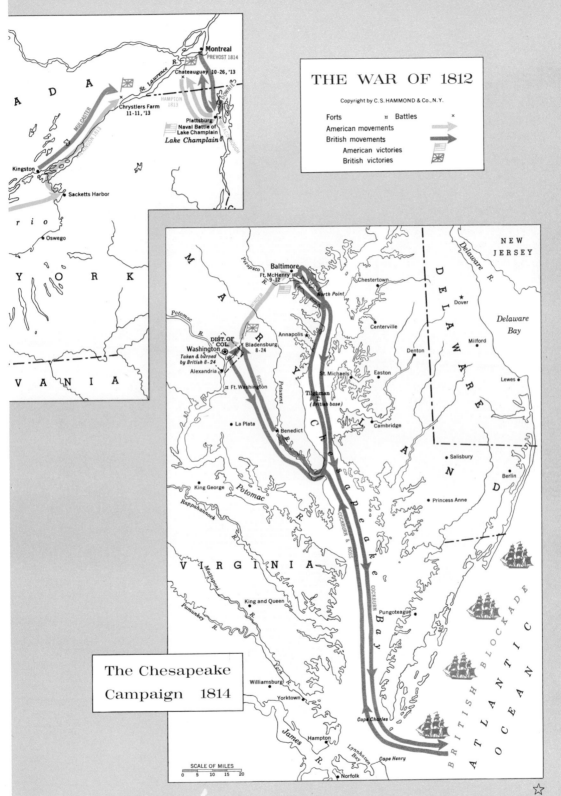

THE WAR OF 1812

Copyright by C.S. HAMMOND & Co., N.Y.

Forts ¤ Battles ×
American movements →
British movements →
American victories
British victories

The Chesapeake Campaign 1814

Inset map (upper left)

Montreal
PREVOST 1814
Chateauguay 10-26, '13
HAMPTON 1813
St. Lawrence R.
Chrystlers Farm 11-11, '13
WILKINSON 1813
MULCASTER
Plattsburg
Naval Battle of Lake Champlain
Lake Champlain
Kingston
Sacketts Harbor
Oswego
CANADA
NEW YORK
PENNSYLVANIA
Ontario

Main map

NEW JERSEY
Delaware R.
Dover
Delaware Bay
Chestertown
Centerville
Milford
Denton
Lewes
Salisbury
Berlin
Princess Anne
Pungoteague
DELAWARE
MARYLAND

MARYLAND
Patapsco
Baltimore
Ft. McHenry 9-12
North Point
Annapolis
St. Michaels
Easton
Cambridge
Tilghman (British base)
Potomac R.
DIST. OF COL.
Washington
Taken & burned by British 8-24
Bladensburg 8-24
Alexandria
Ft. Washington
Patuxent R.
La Plata
Benedict
King George
Potomac R.
Rappahannock R.
Chesapeake Bay
COCKBURN & ROSS
COCKBURN

VIRGINIA
Mattaponi R.
Pamunkey R.
King and Queen
Williamsburg
Yorktown
Hampton
York R.
James R.
Lynnhaven Bay
Cape Charles
Cape Henry
Norfolk
BRITISH BLOCKADE
ATLANTIC OCEAN

SCALE OF MILES
0 5 10 15 20

☆ 67

into the bay to bring an exchanged prisoner to shore, and could not get back because of the battle. "By the dawn's early light" he saw the American flag still bravely flying on the ramparts of the fort! Francis Scott Key was so moved that he wrote THE STAR-SPANGLED BANNER, and it became our national anthem.

After the burning of Washington, the country was so angry that President Madison was able to arouse a strong will to win. As the war continued, resistance grew and was organized. It spread into the south, and along the Gulf of Mexico. There "Old Hickory" Andrew Jackson had defeated the Creek Indians, and was now bringing in frontiersmen to join his troops and his own Indian allies. He marched his army toward New Orleans to defend a city soon to be attacked by a British fleet, which had just been released from a war with France.

New Orleans was a gay place. Soft breezes blew across the city a scent of jasmine mixed with rich Creole cooking. In narrow streets, overhung by balconies, French chatter and laughter drowned out the voices of mockingbirds. Citizens did not care that many of their goods were brought in by pirates living downriver at Barataria Bay. Jean Lafitte the buccaneer chief, who plundered merchant ships, seemed safe from arrest. When the governor posted a reward for him, he set the city to chuckling by offering a larger reward for the capture of the governor!

And then a frightened hush fell on New Orleans. The British were sailing in! Citizens enlisted in General Jackson's army. Lafitte, who had been offered a deal by the British, instead chose to join the United States. He marched his pirate crew, armed with muskets and cutlasses, to the battle at Lake Borgne. A ship slipped into the bay to bombard the British encampment. Frontiersmen from Tennessee and Kentucky moved like panthers into the night to stalk John Bull as if he were a wild animal prey. They caught sentries and tomahawked them. By day, while pirates fought with no quarter, Andy Jackson's cannon blasted the enemy's mud redoubts.

On January 8, 1815, a crucial battle was fought just outside of New Orleans. When the British stormed the American line of defense they were thrown back and their commander was killed. Enemy troops retreated to their ships and sailed away. Louisiana was too far away to know it, but this battle was fought two weeks after a peace treaty had been signed at Ghent, Belgium. The United States was safe. Now men turned eager eyes to the west.

TRAILS TO THE WEST

12

Crisscrossing America there were ancient trails trodden bare by the moccasined feet of Indians. Settlers followed the Wilderness and the Cumberland roads west over the mountains — and the Old Warrior Path led from Kentucky up to Lake Erie. The Ohio River was another route westward, and great migrations floated on it in flatboats and on rafts.

Daniel Boone found Kentucky too crowded for him after a while. He took his family beyond the Mississippi into the Missouri wilderness. Boone and his sons boiled salt from a "salt lick" and took it down by boat to sell in a tiny French village called St. Louis. Old Daniel complained that, although he kept moving, people came right along behind him. In Missouri he said that he hoped to find rest — "but I was still pursued — for I had not been two years at the licks before a damned Yankee came and settled down within a hundred miles of me."

Near Wilderness Road the terrible Harpe family waited for victims. Soon after the Revolution Big and Little Harpe, their mother, and savage wives, would leap like fiends from the forest on travelers. At last, when the Kentucky countryside was so aroused that posses scoured the woods for the murderers, the Harpes escaped to the Mississippi River. There they joined other outlaws living in a lair called Cave-in-Rock, overlooking the river. From this hideout river pirates swooped out upon luckless riders on rafts and flatboats. It wasn't long before even the pirates hated the Harpes and drove them out. A year later the law caught up with them, Big Harpe was killed and Little Harpe disappeared. The women were tried and acquitted. Sometimes frontier justice missed its mark!

Along the Mississippi the Natchez Trace was dangerous, also. After a farmer had floated his grain and pigs down the river and sold them in New Orleans he rode back with money in his saddlebags. He stopped in horror on the Natchez Trace, for lying on the trail was the body of a victim of the ruthless Murrell gang. He knew that he would be lucky to finish his own journey safely, even with his shotgun held ready on the pommel of his saddle.

Across the Mississippi and beyond the Missouri, trails wound to the north,

ROUTES TO THE WEST
1760-1860

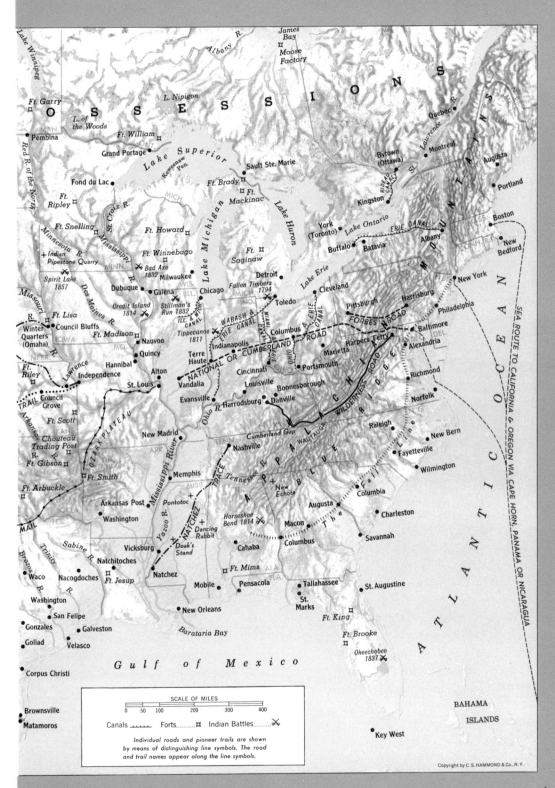

BRITISH POSSESSIONS

Lake Winnipeg

Albany R.

James Bay
Moose Factory

Ft. Garry
L. Nipigon

L. of the Woods

Pembina

Red R. of the North

Grand Portage

Ft. William
ONT.

Lake Superior

Keweenaw Pen.

Sault Ste. Marie

Quebec
Augusta

MOUNTAINS

St. Lawrence R.

Montreal

Bytown (Ottawa)

RIDEAU CANAL

Portland

Fond du Lac

Ft. Ripley
MICH.

Ft. Brady

Ft. Mackinac

Kingston

Boston

Ft. Snelling

St. Croix R.

Mississippi R.

Minnesota R.

MINN.

Indian Pipestone Quarry

Spirit Lake 1857

Ft. Howard

Ft. Winnebago

Bad Axe 1832

Lake Michigan

Lake Huron

Ft. Saginaw

Milwaukee

York (Toronto)

Lake Ontario

ERIE CANAL

Albany

Buffalo

Batavia

CONN. R.I.

New Bedford

New York

Des Moines R.

Dubuque
WIS.

Galena
ILL.

Chicago

Detroit

Fallen Timbers 1794
MICH.
IND.

Lake Erie

Cleveland

Pittsburgh

Harrisburg

Philadelphia

Missouri R.

Ft. Lisa

Winter Quarters (Omaha)

Council Bluffs
IOWA

Ft. Madison
MO.

Credit Island 1814

Stillman's Run 1832
ILL. & MICH. CANAL

Nauvoo

WABASH & ERIE CANAL

Tippecanoe 1811

Columbus

MIAMI & ERIE CANAL

Toledo

OHIO & ERIE CANAL

FORBES ROAD

Baltimore
DEL.
MD.

Alexandria

Harpers Ferry

Ft. Riley
NEBR.

Lawrence
KANS.

Independence

Hannibal

Quincy

Indianapolis

Terre Haute

Vandalia

OHIO R.

Marietta

Portsmouth

Richmond

Norfolk

NATIONAL OR CUMBERLAND ROAD

Cincinnati

Louisville

Boonesborough

WILDERNESS ROAD

VA.

TRAIL

Council Grove

Ft. Scott

Chouteau Trading Post
KANS.

Ft. Gibson

Ft. Arbuckle

Arkansas R.

Ft. Smith

OKLA.
TEX.

New Madrid

Alton

St. Louis

Evansville

Harrodsburg

Ohio R.

Danville

Cumberland Gap

Nashville
TENN.

Memphis
MISS.

APPALACHIAN

WAUTAUGA

BLUE RIDGE

Raleigh

New Bern

Fayetteville

Wilmington

MAIL

Sabine R.

Brazos R.

Trinity R.

Waco

Nacogdoches

Washington

San Felipe

Gonzales

Goliad

Galveston

Velasco

Corpus Christi

Brownsville

Matamoros

Natchitoches

Ft. Jesup

Vicksburg

Yazoo R.

Mississippi River

NATCHEZ TRACE

Pontotoc

Doak's Stand

Natchez

Arkansas Post

Washington
ARK.

OZARK PLATEAU

Dancing Rabbit

Horseshoe Bend 1814

Cahaba

New Echota

Columbus

Macon

Augusta

Columbia

The Fall Line

Charleston

Savannah

ENG.

Mobile

Pensacola

ALA.
FLA.

Ft. Mims

Tallahassee

St. Marks

St. Augustine

New Orleans

Barataria Bay

Ft. King

Ft. Brooke

Okeechobee 1837

ATLANTIC OCEAN

SEA ROUTE TO CALIFORNIA & OREGON VIA CAPE HORN, PANAMA OR NICARAGUA

Gulf of Mexico

BAHAMA ISLANDS

Key West

SCALE OF MILES

0 50 100   200   300   400

Canals ⌐⌐⌐⌐   Forts .... ⌐   Indian Battles .... ✕

Individual roads and pioneer trails are shown by means of distinguishing line symbols. The road and trail names appear along the line symbols.

Copyright by C. S. HAMMOND & Co., N.Y.

to the Rocky Mountains, and southward to Spanish country. All kinds of people took these trails — hunter, trapper, scout, Indian fighter, and outlaw. There were also buffalo skinners and mule drivers. After some years along came the cowmen, settlers, lawmen, and school teachers.

For 780 miles across the plains the Santa Fe Trail stretched its dusty length to the southwestern country. There were no high mountains or big streams to cross. Horses were soon followed by long lines of mule or ox drawn wagons. In earlier times the town of Santa Fe, rich in silver and wool, had to get supplies all the way from Veracruz, Mexico. This was over a long route through Apache country. Americans weren't allowed to trade in Santa Fe. Then William Becknell opened up the Santa Fe Trail from Independence, Missouri, across the prairies and plains to the old Spanish-Indian city in New Mexico. Another fork of this trail turned north to Bent's Fort, a trading post in the Rocky Mountains foothills.

Wagons moving slowly by day on the Santa Fe Trail drew into a circle for protection against Indian attack at night. Columns of cavalry, on the way to distant outposts, kerchiefs flying, passed the transport wagons. Bleached bones of animals caught the scorching sun along the route. Mail and stagecoaches dashed by settlers and miners on horses, and in Conestoga wagons.

"There goes the stage!" Baggage bouncing, passengers hanging to straps to keep from hitting the roof, driver leaning forward, whip cracking, shouting, "Glang. Haw! Haw!"

Oregon country was an Indian land of mountain and rich valley, of wild fruits, game, and streams choked with fish. John Jacob Astor had built Astoria, his beaverpelt trading post, in this region. To it came Marcus and Narcissa Whitman, missionaries, in 1836. Narcissa was the first white woman to make the long journey to Oregon. Only a few years later she and her husband were killed by marauding Cayuse Indians.

The trail to Oregon led across and beyond the Great American Desert, as the Great Plains were then called. It was soon followed by settlers, plodding slowly along. After a while the hooves of horses and oxen, and the wheels of wagons made a deep rutted road. Along the way there were piles of bones of cattle and oxen and hundreds of graves of those who did not reach the end of the trail. Some had died fighting hostile Indians, and others of deadly cholera. The main part of this trail was also the route for gold seekers heading for California, and for Mormons fleeing persecution. Led by Brigham Young these Latter Day Saints were searching for their own kingdom. They settled in Salt Lake City, Utah. Hundreds, thousands, and tens of thousands of people took that trail to the west.

Wells Fargo was the first large express company in the west. It began in 1852, and ten years later it had taken on ocean service, made its headquarters in booming San Francisco, and was operating all over the Pacific coast region, as well as across plains and mountains. The Butterfield Mail stagecoaches, on the Ox-bow Route from the Mississippi River, through the southwest to Los Angeles and San Francisco, carried mail and express for Wells Fargo. By 1861 Wells Fargo owned most of the Butterfield Company. On its many routes it carried more gold and silver than any other agency, and was famous for its daring stage drivers, its shotgun riders protecting treasure boxes, and its safe mail delivery even to distant mining towns. When railroads came to crisscross western lands Wells Fargo sent express shipments by rail, and put shotgun guards on baggage cars to protect boxes of gold and silver from bandits.

Everyone thought the Butterfield Mail made fast time on a twenty-two day run from St. Louis, Missouri, to Los Angeles, California. And then on an April day in 1860 the Pony Express was off on the northern trail, from St. Joseph, Missouri. A rider flung himself on his fast horse and with saddlebags flapping he pounded across the plains. At the first way station a fresh rider and horse were waiting. Without stopping, the bag of mail was thrown from one rider to the next, who disappeared to the west. Nothing stopped the Pony Express. Some riders were killed by Comanche arrows, but there were others ready to take the mail on its way. The best time for a run from Fort Kearney to Fort Churchill, Nebraska, was six days, when the Pony Express took the news of the election of President Lincoln.

In the second year of the service, poles were put up across the plains and over the mountains, and crackling telegraph wires were strung. There were no horses fast enough to compete with the telegraph in carrying the news, and no riders strong and daring enough to get there ahead of it. The Pony Express went out of business after eighteen months of this incredible means of communication. The riders hung up their saddlebags and took on other jobs, ending one of the most thrilling activities in western history.

Woodcut, 1861 by G. H. Andrews   *The Bettmann Archive*

THE PONY EXPRESS

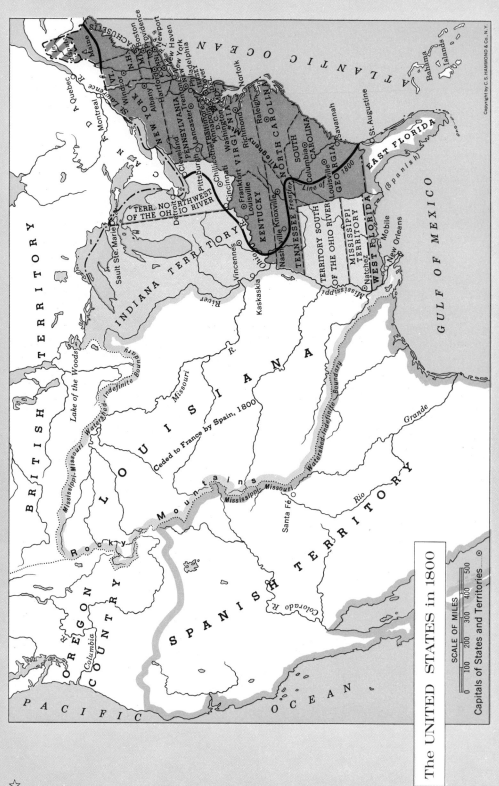

The UNITED STATES in 1800

SCALE OF MILES
0   100   200   300   400   500

Capitals of States and Territories ⊙

Copyright by C. S. HAMMOND & Co., N.Y.

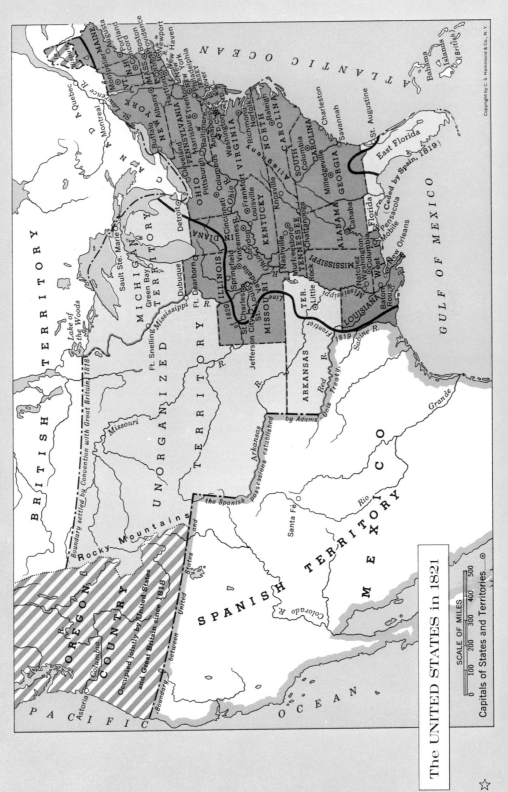

The UNITED STATES in 1821

SCALE OF MILES

0   100   200   300   400   500

Capitals of States and Territories......⊙

Copyright by C. S. Hammond & Co., N. Y.

PIONEERS AND EXPLORERS

13 Eastern excitement rose high with canal building after 1800.

"I've got a mule, her name is Sal, fifteen miles on the Erie Canal!"

The Erie Canal was completed in 1825 by DeWitt Clinton. Through the Mohawk Valley, once echoing to the war cries of the Iroquois, blunt-nosed barges were hauled at three miles an hour by mules plodding along the towpath. The barges resembled bright birds seen just above green meadows and waving marsh grasses. Passengers sat on their decks, the ladies with lacy parasols protecting them from the sun. The travelers often sang lively tunes. On freight barges men minded their goods and women minded their children. Twenty thousand barges a season moved from Buffalo to New York and back. The Erie Canal became the pathway to the old Northwest. It opened the country to trade and settlement, and brought a flood of people into the Great Lakes region.

At Buffalo settlers left canal boats and went down Lake Erie to the tall forests of Michigan and Indiana. These trees were two to five feet around their trunks, and so high that sunlight could not penetrate their tops to the tangled undergrowth beneath. At first travel had to be on the water, for cutting through tough wild vines and piled up dead trees was impossible. On the land Indian tribes had long ago found the few easy trails.

As a new century dawned for the new nation, in 1800, Ohio Territory was divided from Indiana, and the old Northwest pushed beyond the Mississippi. Indiana stretched from forest to prairie, and up to Canada. Even after people came into the territory by the Erie Canal and Great Lakes route a borderer there was half-hunter and half-farmer. With aching toil he cleared a small piece of land, axing trees, grubbing stumps, firing them out, or planting around them. He found fish for the taking in clear creeks — and he paused with hoe in hand to stretch his neck back and watch clouds of birds wing across the sky. His gun could bring in bear, deer, or wild turkeys for good eating with corn pone. Squatters who moved in without paying for land floated down the Ohio from eastern Pennsylvania. Up from Kentucky they came on an old trail. "Go along there," they shouted to their horses or oxen as they crossed creeks in flood. They fixed their eyes resolutely ahead of them day by day. Through the night children shivered at wolf's howl and panther's scream. At dawn pioneer wagons rolled onward again.

Crack went the long bull whips! Shouts and cries! Calls to the youngest "shirttail boys" who were running with their dogs alongside packhorses. Perched on the wagon, with her cat curled comfortably on the best feather-bed, was mother. Granny was there too, mending a pair of linsey-woolsey breeches for son, who was striding before the team at a slow mile-eating jog. Behind the driver, in the wagon bed, a cherished dresser rode beside a few homemade cane-bottomed chairs. The cradle rocked gently close to one of the girls so that she could look after the baby sleeping inside. A water barrel, tied with leather thongs, thumped the side of the wagon.

When several families moved together there might be a hoedown one night, fiddle racing, and young Johnny doing a buck-and-wing on the tailgate of the Conestoga wagon. In Indiana the thud of ax blade on tree trunk and the crash of falling trees startled flocks of birds. At first a family lived in an opensided shelter, sometimes all winter, with snow drifting in. The raising of a log cabin was an event. Neighbors rode in from a hundred miles around to lend their muscles. Sometimes newcomers lived in dug-out rooms underground for several years before the land was cleared, a few fields planted, and a tiny cabin and barn constructed.

Life was hard and death always nearby. Yet the coming of summer meant trips for wild berries and honey, quilting bees and all day church gatherings. In winter, almost hidden under snowdrifts, cabins were kept warm, and chestnuts were roasted in the fireplace of an evening. The wife brought along a small sack of apple and gourd seeds. Gourds made cups, bowls, and dippers for the spring, and soft soap could be stored in them. The women tied brooms of hickory twigs. But their most valued possessions were iron cooking pots to swing over the hob on an open fireplace. Pioneers had a few knives, but seldom forks. Fingers were plenty good enough.

Thomas Lincoln journeyed from Kentucky to the Indiana wilderness. With him were his wife Nancy, their daughter Sarah, and Abraham, of the thin frame, bony face, and shaggy black hair. The Lincolns spent their first cold winter in a lean-to listening to wild animals prowling close by. Thomas' first cabin had one room, with a ladder to a loft up under the hand-split shingles. When pale green clouds of new leaf were on every tree, Thomas Sparrow and family, kinfolks, arrived from Kentucky. Grief came with them, for the Sparrows soon died of a sickness. Not long after that Nancy took sick, too. Soon Abe must stand with his sister and father beside his mother's lonely grave in the forest.

Pioneers moved south as well as north from the thirteen states. They cracked their long whips down into Georgia, Alabama, and Florida. Sometimes they were attacked by fierce Creeks, Cherokees, or Seminoles. Sometimes they, too, savagely attacked Indian villages, killing women and children as well as braves. Some frontiersmen going north, south, and west were as ferocious as panthers. They looked on the Indian as if he were a wild animal to be destroyed on sight, without waiting to find out if he might be friendly. Some borderers took Indian scalps and turned them over to the government for bounty money.

At the beginning of the nineteenth century Spain still ruled in Mexico, Florida, California, and the whole southwest. Spaniards had come to settle California and the southwest before the American Revolution. In 1769, Spanish authorities decided to make a permanent claim to California by sending an expedition to the north from Lower California. This plan had two objectives: to establish Christianity under the Catholic Church of Spain, and to place military posts in California.

Three ships sailed, loaded with tools, seeds, household goods, sacred objects, and vestments. A land expedition set out, also, led by two army captains. Father Junipero Serra headed the group of Franciscan monks who traveled by land. They went on foot, the two groups driving herds of cattle along with them. Their first stop, after a difficult journey, was at San Diego, where Father Serra founded a mission. Then they pushed on in one group through brush and forests and rocky mountainous country. The little column of Indians, monks in brown robes, Spanish officers with their bright uniforms and soldiers clad in leather wound slowly northward until they reached a great bay, which they called San Francisco. There, and at Monterey, they built little missions, planted gardens and a few fields, and erected small forts, called presidios. California had been secured with the cross and the royal standard of Spain.

Spaniards were given huge grants of land, both in California and in the Arizona and New Mexico regions, which had been settled much earlier. These Spanish caballeros built haciendas and princely ranches, stocked with fine horses. Their vaqueros, or cowboys, rode herd on thousands of cattle and became some of the best horsemen of the world. They held rodeos to exhibit their skill as riders, and on the ranches fiestas were gay with music and dancing, lasting for days at a time. Across the southwest mission bells tolled in church towers. Indians were worked as slaves both at missions and on ranches.

The town of Santa Fe, New Mexico, was founded in 1609, only two years after the English colony landed at Jamestown, Virginia. Spain gradually grew weaker in Europe, but for a long time she continued to prosper in America, and regarded Mexico and the southwestern part of North America as her possession. Yet Mexico, so long under the domination of Spain, was growing independent. After she had thrown off her Spanish conqueror, Mexico claimed California and the southwest for herself.

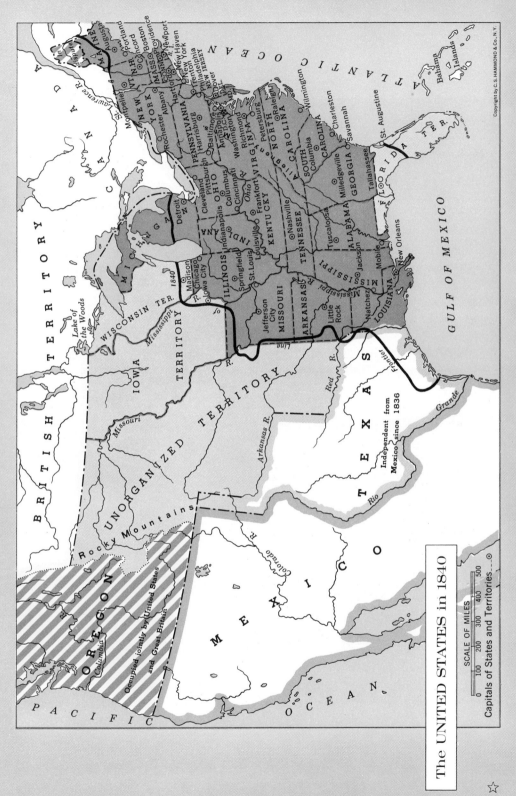

The UNITED STATES in 1840

SCALE OF MILES

0 100 200 300 400 500

Capitals of States and Territories....◉

AMERICANS INVADE MEXICO

14 Texans, in 1821, paid very little attention to news of the Mexican revolution. Spanish or Mexican, what difference did it make? The southwest was a long way from Mexico City. What the Mexicans did not think of for a while, but soon were forced to recognize, was that men were coming west from the United States. These were energetic, fighting men who wanted a share in Texas land. Under big Sam Houston they joined forces to take Texas from Mexico. By 1835 Houston and his Texans had swept Mexican troops out of some of their forts.

General Santa Anna, dictator of Mexico, had no intention of letting the province of Texas escape him. He prepared his army for an invasion. In the winter of 1836 Santa Anna moved up to San Antonio, where a defiant little group of Americans held the Alamo Mission. Houston wasn't with them. Inside the thick walls this band of fighting men was led by Davy Crockett, Bill Travis, and Jim Bowie, who had invented the famous two-edged knife. They refused to surrender. Their grim resolution was, "Victory or death!"

After dark on the eighth day of siege thirty-two volunteers crept through Mexican lines into the mission. Even with these reinforcements there were fewer than two hundred inside the Alamo. They were all sleepless, hungry, and their ammunition was running low; but they held out for no surrender.

At dawn Mexican troops stormed the walls, and then fell back. Soon came another assault! Inside of the walls Jim Bowie had been disabled, and others were dead or wounded. At last the wall was breached. Hand-to-hand fighting raged through the mission. Davy Crockett and his twelve Tennesseans fell inside the church, which was captured last. The Mexicans had lost nearly fifteen hundred troops.

"Remember the Alamo!" became a cry that swept the west.

At San Jacinto Texans fought with this cry, and won. Sam Houston descended on Santa Anna's camp as the general was taking his siesta. The Mexican general fled, still wearing his red carpet slippers. Later, Sam Houston found his quarry hiding among the wild grasses not far away.

Texas became an independent republic, with Sam Houston as president.

In 1845, the Lone Star flag came down and the Stars and Stripes went up. Texas was admitted to the Union as the twenty-eighth state.

The annexation of Texas by the United States in 1845 was looked on in Mexico as a declaration of war. Mexico withdrew her ambassador from Washington and severed diplomatic relations. At this action hotheads in Congress and throughout the United States cried out for war with Mexico. Yet the American government was trying to preserve peace by diplomatic means, and President Polk was working on a plan to try to purchase California. Mexico refused to reopen relations, however, and instead sent an army to the Rio Grande River, which formed the boundary with Texas. President Polk ordered General Zachary Taylor to move with all speed to the river. The battle of Matamoros was won by the Americans, who then moved down into Mexico. General Taylor took his troops deeper into the country, through the bleak Sierra Madre Mountains, and across a snake and scorpion ridden desert. American soldiers, under General Doniphan, approached Monterrey.

Monterrey was a strongly fortified city, but the American troops succeeded in bringing a surrender after a fierce assault on its defenses. In the following year the Mexican army under General Santa Anna made a stand at Buena Vista. This battle was fought so well by the Mexicans that, although they lost, in Washington it was decided to attempt to reach Mexico City by a landing on the Gulf of Mexico coast instead of continuing from the north. A fleet transported troops to Veracruz

and General Winfield Scott was given command of the army. Among his junior officers were young Stonewall Jackson, Ulysses Grant, William T. Sherman, Joseph Johnston, and G. T. Beauregard.

Although the fortress of San Juan de Ulúa was defended by fifty-two cannon, it surrendered under bombardment. American soldiers could look up at the snowcapped peak of Mount Orizaba as they made their way deep into Mexico on the route taken so long before by Cortez. Would wily Santa Anna command the road with batteries on the cliffs? Scott must strike the Mexican army from the rear. A young lieutenant went swiftly out into rocky, cactus country to spy out the land. Suffering from insects, thirst, and heat he slipped forward by night, and hid by day. His reports brought a victory at Cerro Gordo, and put the Mexicans to flight. Santa Anna, who had lost a leg and had it buried with honors in Mexico City, forgot his wooden leg in his hasty retreat.

The American lieutenant was promoted to the rank of major for his skill and daring. He stared down on the vast lava field before the Mexican city. Over there in a high valley guarded by lofty mountains was the ancient capital, once the stronghold of the Emperor Montezuma. It was heavily fortified with stone forts and walls, and the officer knew that inside there were stronger Mexican forces than the Americans commanded. Mexico City must be taken from the rear, and by complete surprise.

Once more the major was sent out on a scouting expedition. Before an assault could be made on the city, out-

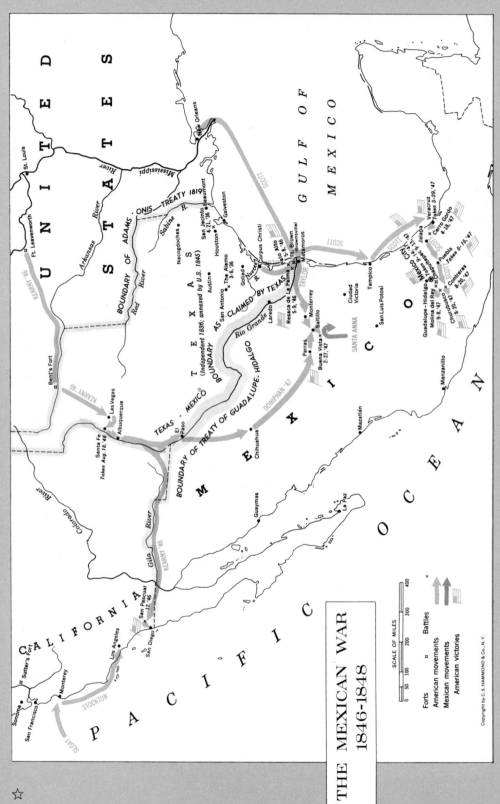

THE MEXICAN WAR
1846-1848

SCALE OF MILES

| 0 | 50 | 100 | 200 | 300 | 400 |

Forts
American movements
Mexican movements
American victories

× Battles

Copyright by C. S. HAMMOND & Co., N. Y.

posts must be captured. He led a little force across the jagged black lava field, called the Pedegral, to the village of San Geronimo. The general in command did not have enough men to take it, and so the major once more crossed the Pedegral and brought in reinforcements. The outpost was taken. For a fourth time the major crossed the lava rocks and then, without rest, he went into battle at Churubusco.

After that fight had been won General Scott called these crossings of the Pedegral the "greatest feat of physical and moral courage performed by an individual in the war with Mexico." The major was Robert E. Lee.

American troops stormed the ancient castle of Chapultepec, on the Hill of Grasshoppers, outside Mexico City. This was a military school for young cadets, and was now defended by Mexican soldiers. On a September day, in bursts of rain and sunlight, Americans crossed the moat and opened fire. Braving heavy cannonading they climbed the walls and in hand-to-hand fighting battled the defenders on top of the parapets.

Mexican cadets fought like men in this battle. When one boy realized that the Mexicans were losing he grasped a flag and jumped over the parapet to his death. This assault is called the "Battle of the Brave Boys," and is one of the heroic events in Mexican history.

Mexico City surrendered. Once more Santa Anna fled, and the American invaders were victorious. The United States and Mexico signed a peace treaty. Robert E. Lee was promoted to the rank of colonel. The United States gained the Arizona, New Mexico, western Colorado, Utah, Nevada, and California territories. Mexico was paid fifteen million dollars for them.

Even before the Mexican War ended Americans had their eyes on California. Captain John C. Fremont, "Pathfinder of the West," led a group of American settlers to revolt against Mexican authorities. They took a military post and then raised a flag proclaiming the "California Republic." In this "Bear Flag Revolution" the Mexicans were winning. Then Colonel Kearney led an army in from the southwest and, with Fremont and Commodore Stockton, won the struggle. The independent state was short-lived, however, for at the end of the Mexican War California joined the United States as a territory.

Now all that was needed to bring Americans there in full force was an unknown carpenter who picked some shining pebbles from the bed of a little known stream.

THERE'S GOLD IN CALIFORNIA!

15

January — 1848! James Marshall, carpenter, was building a millrace in the American River, in northern California. With a handful of gravel and a few golden nuggets, he went to see his employer. John Sutter, the Swiss who owned so many rich acres that he thought of it as his "kingdom," wasn't much interested in a handful of gold. Others were! The news flashed from Sutter's ranch to Sacramento, and on to San Francisco. Gold! Gold on the American River! Word was carried on horseback through ranchland. It spread by ship out of San Francisco Bay and to distant shores. Men headed for Sutter's. John Sutter, the slow-speaking rancher, grew angry and tried to run these interlopers off.

As fast as he chased them from his property they came back, and in greater numbers. Men squatted in cold river water, shaking shallow pans around and around to slosh out sand and leave the heavier gold dust and nuggets. "Oh, Susanna, now don't you cry for me, for I'm off to Cal-i-forni-a with a banjo on my knee!" John Sutter, living like a baron, was ruined. And still they came!

In ports around the world gold fever gripped men. They called California, El Dorado — land of glittering fortune! Shipping companies printed circulars, and men rushed to ships. Any old vessel that could be found was put into service and jammed with gold seekers jabbering in a mixture of languages. Every man believed that he would become a millionaire. Some ships took the long, hard voyage around Cape Horn, and were buffeted by the violent storms that blew at the tip of South America. Tossed about and sick these "argonauts" at last sailed up the coast to the bay of San Francisco.

Others went across the Isthmus of Panama. Vessels dumped them on the tropical shore, where they had to make their way on foot, or on the backs of mules or donkeys, to the Pacific coast. They waded through swamps and if they survived, they came out to be picked up by unseaworthy tramp ships and taken to California.

Only a brief yesterday away San Francisco had been a tiny Mexican village called *Yerba Buena*. Now its steep hills overlooking the magnificent bay were alive with gold rushers, and echoed with shouts and the clatter of ships unloading. The town was a vast banging of sawing and hammering, as shacks went up by the hundreds. The streets were either enveloped in clouds of dust, or were swamps of mud, in which mules and wagons could sink to destruction. Men of all nationalities jammed the crude plank sidewalks. They wore red flannel shirts, trousers stuffed into boots, and wide hats. They all carried picks and pans slung over their shoulders, and looked alike in their beards. Yet in this throng there were lawyers, preachers, doctors, clerks, and businessmen, as well as laborers and lumberjacks. Those who wore broadcloth and high hats were usually gamblers and confidence men. Every few feet along the streets there were small-time thieves. Some had shell games set up on boxes.

"Watch the little pea, gentlemen! Now, which little walnut shell has the little pea?"

At night a huge field of tents, spread over the chaparral covered hills, bloomed with kerosene lanterns and candles until the city glowed like a cluster of moons. Noise was as great at night as in the day. Every gambling tent or shack was a crush of men losing their pokes of gold dust and nuggets. Gold was everywhere. Owners of saloons panned gold dust out of the sawdust on the floors. It was said that even in the barbering tents gold dust was collected from the snipped whiskers.

In 1849 the greatest migration of fortune hunters the world had ever seen came to California. Cowhands deserted ranches for the goldfields. Crops were not harvested. The cost of food in San Francisco rose sky-high. A dollar an egg! Ten dollars per dinner! A miner paid it, or he cooked his own beans and sowbelly bacon to eat with his saleratus biscuits. And he paid high prices for bacon and beans, too.

Across the land they struggled westward in a flood that later included women and children. Until the wagons came creaking down the mountain passes into California, miners had seen few women there. They would drop pick and pan and walk miles just to stare and say, "Howdy, ma'am." Any child looked like an angel to them. Little Lotta Crabtree, of the dancing feet and sweet voice, came to entertain in Hangtown, Git-Up-And-Git, Red Dog Camp, and Murderer's Bar. The applause for her was punctuated with the thump of gold pokes hitting the stage floor. Tears ran down the faces of bearded miners as they looked at the small child.

The trek across the Great Plains and mountains was rough and dangerous. Long wagon trains were fairly safe from Indian attack, but small parties were often raided and their horses stolen. These forty-niners from north, east, south, and foreign lands all headed out into buffalo and Indian country. From Pike County, Arkansas, they started west, too.

"Oh, don't you remember sweet Betsy from Pike,
Who crossed the big mountains with her lover Ike,
With two yoke of oxen, a large yellow dog,
A tall Shanghai rooster, and one spotted hog."

At first miners dug and panned. Then they made sluice boxes called

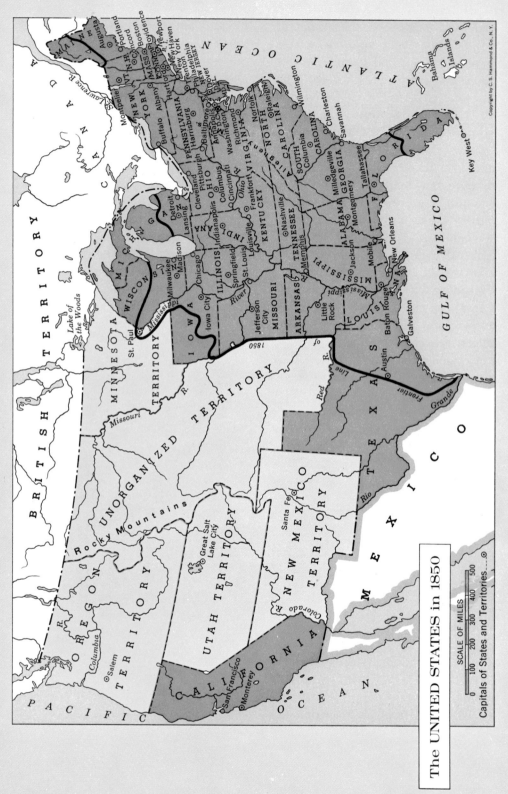

The UNITED STATES in 1850

SCALE OF MILES

0 100 200 300 400 500

Capitals of States and Territories......◎

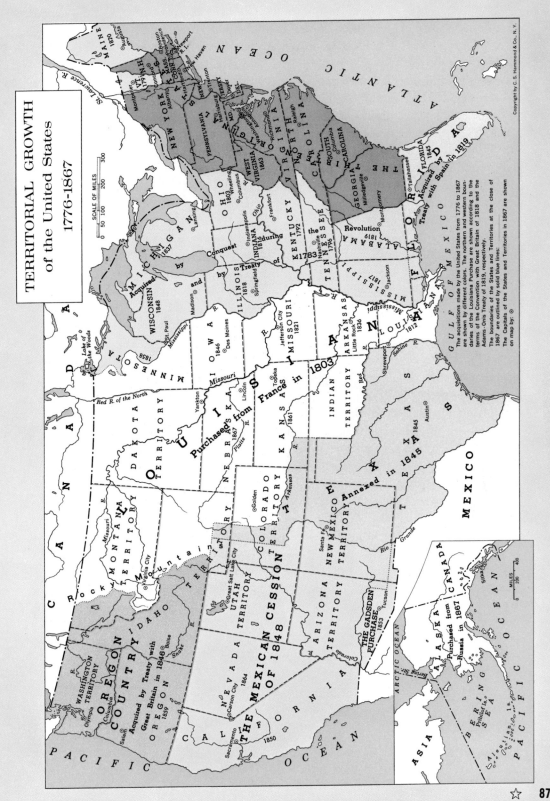

TERRITORIAL GROWTH
of the United States
1776-1867

SCALE OF MILES
0 50 100 200 300

Copyright by C. S. Hammond & Co., N.Y.

The acquisitions made by the United States from 1776 to 1867 are shown by different colors. The northern and western boundaries of the Louisiana Purchase are shown according to the terms of the Convention with Great Britain of 1818 and the Adams-Onis Treaty of 1819, respectively.

The boundaries of the States and Territories at the close of 1867 are outlined by solid blue lines.

The Capitals of the States and Territories in 1867 are shown on map by: ⊙

ATLANTIC OCEAN

CANADA

MEXICO

PACIFIC OCEAN

GULF OF MEXICO

MAINE 1820

NEW YORK

PENNSYLVANIA

WEST VIRGINIA 1863

VIRGINIA

NORTH CAROLINA

SOUTH CAROLINA

GEORGIA

FLORIDA Acquired by Treaty with Spain in 1819

THE FLORIDAS

OHIO 1803

MICHIGAN 1837

Acquired by Conquest and by Treaty of 1783 during the Revolution

KENTUCKY 1792

TENNESSEE 1796

INDIANA 1816

ILLINOIS 1818

WISCONSIN 1848

MISSISSIPPI 1817

ALABAMA 1819

MINNESOTA 1858

IOWA 1846

MISSOURI 1821

ARKANSAS 1836

LOUISIANA 1812

Purchased from France in 1803

DAKOTA TERRITORY

NEBRASKA 1867

KANSAS 1861

INDIAN TERRITORY

TEXAS Annexed in 1845

COLORADO TERRITORY

NEW MEXICO TERRITORY

MEXICO

MONTANA TERRITORY

IDAHO TERRITORY

UTAH TERRITORY

ARIZONA TERRITORY

THE GADSDEN PURCHASE 1853

THE MEXICAN CESSION OF 1848

NEVADA 1864

CALIFORNIA 1850

OREGON COUNTRY

WASHINGTON TERRITORY

OREGON 1859

Acquired by Treaty with Great Britain in 1846

Rocky Mountains

ALASKA Purchased from CANADA Russia in 1867

ARCTIC OCEAN

BERING SEA

PACIFIC OCEAN

ASIA

MILES 0 200 400

☆ **87**

long toms — into which they dumped gravel and poured water. The water ran gravel out, leaving gold caught in the wooden riffles. Then two men discovered that they could wash down hillsides easier with hoses. After a few years of mining the banks of streams and hills were scarred and pitted, with ugly mounds of dirt and stone piled up along them. Trees were uprooted and forests ruined.

At the beginning camps were honest and a prospector could leave his poke anywhere without fear of theft. Miners had their own code of law and honor. If a theft or murder did take place they dealt with the crime in a "miner's court." But the gold fever began to bring in toughs. Towns were lawless, with shootings on the streets, and claim jumping in the diggings. Chinese, in their blue gowns and pigtails, were victimized by "salted claims," when a crook put a bit of gold dust into the earth and then told the "sucker" to dig in that spot. On the highways bandits lay in wait to rob a miner on his way to town.

The most daring bandit of the gold rush was Joachin Murrieta. He was a law abiding Mexican citizen until he was subjected to brutal and unprovoked treatment by miners from the United States. After that Murrieta waylaid invaders of the Mexican land of California, and put on a little war against Americans. First of all he set out to get revenge on those who had mistreated him, and it was said that he killed every one of them. Then Murrieta became a highwayman, organized a gang and soon was the terror of the mining camps. All sorts of legends and tales grew up about the Mexican, who rode a swift horse and could vanish in an instant after robbing miners of their hard won gold.

By 1852 he was so feared that California put a reward of five thousand dollars on his head. The next year a posse of twenty rangers led by Captain Harry Love surprised Murrieta and his gang in an arroyo in the Coast Range. Three-fingered Jack, the gang's lieutenant, was killed. When the horse was shot from under the famous bandit leader, Murrieta was brought down by a ranger's bullet.

The situation became so bad that vigilante groups took over. But the vigilantes sometimes turned into lawless crowds themselves. As the years passed the rush died out. Fortunes made in the gold diggings were few. Most men who grew rich got their start from selling wheelbarrows, meat, tools, or other necessities. As the gold rush went into big hydraulic mining operations the state settled down. Its climate, farming land, and beauty made it prosperous.

THREATS TO THE NATION

16

While forty-niners were streaming into California to dig for gold Southerners in Congress were insisting that all new territories should be open to slavery. Should new states be slave or free? Northerners shouted for freedom. By 1819 there were equal numbers of slave and free states. Maine was admitted in 1820 as a free state, while Missouri came in without prohibiting slavery. This was called the Missouri Compromise. North of Missouri the rest of the Louisiana Purchase was to be free. By 1848 Congress had passed the Oregon Territory bill forbidding slavery there. California came in as a free state in 1850. This gave one more to the free than to the slavery states. Four years later the Missouri Compromise was repealed by the passage of the Kansas-Nebraska Act.

Was slavery morally right? Everyone had accepted it in the past. The first Negro slaves were brought to Jamestown in 1619 in a Dutch vessel. In the 17th century Swedish ships also took slaves from the Gold Coast of Africa to the Delaware River Valley and to New Amsterdam. Five to ten million African slaves were brought to America between 1619 and 1864. Yankee ships out from New England ports were in the slave trade. Indian slavery was also tried, but did not succeed because Indians so often died in captivity. Except for servants and trained workmen, such as carpenters, slaves did not do well in the North.

On Southern plantations it was a different story. Slave ships unloaded Africans into big shacks called barracoons. As if they were cattle, traders took them out to marketplaces for auction. Slavery was legal in all of the states — but in the fields of the South it was profitable.

In 1792 a young graduate of Yale University came down from the North to live in Georgia. He watched slaves slowly pulling seeds from sticky cotton bolls, and he visualized a machine that could do the job rapidly. From his idea came the cotton gin which played an enormous part in the history of America, although Eli Whitney, its inventor, never made much money out of it. After it came into use, cotton growing became widespread in the South, and plantation owners grew richer from it. King Cotton ruled!

☆ **89**

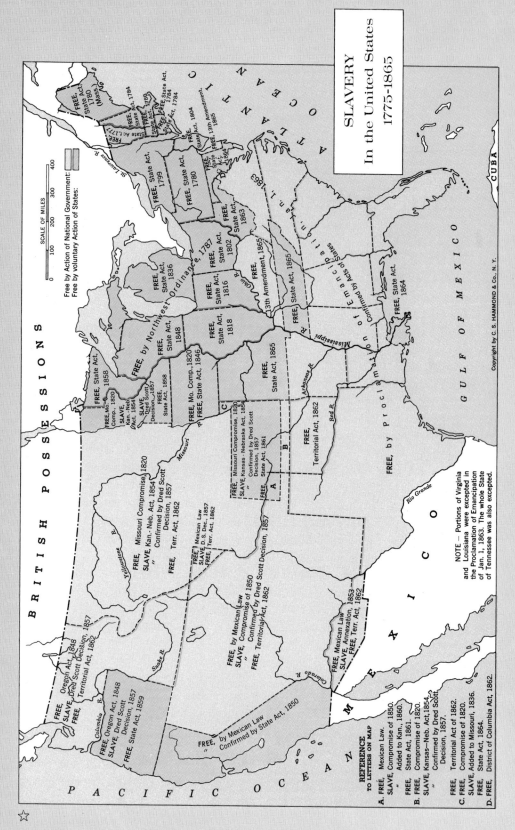

SLAVERY
In the United States
1775-1865

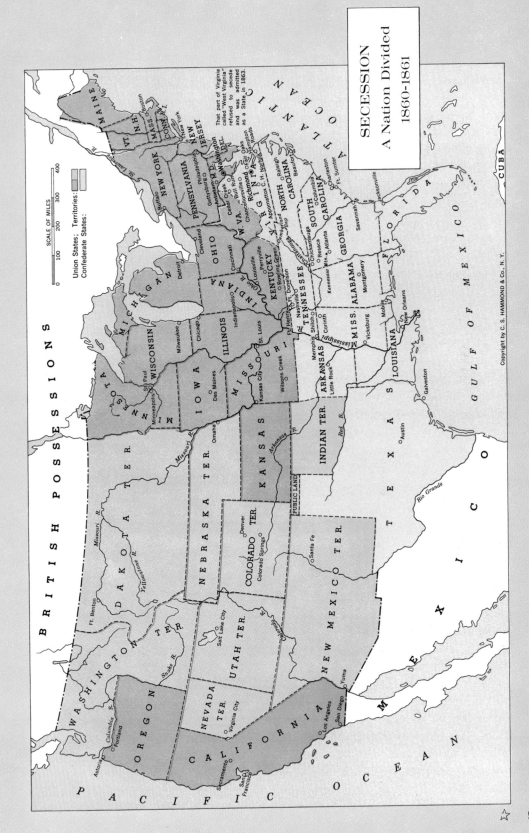

SECESSION
A Nation Divided
1860-1861

Copyright by C. S. HAMMOND & Co., N. Y.

Union States: Territories:
Confederate States:

SCALE OF MILES
0   100   200   300   400

BRITISH POSSESSIONS

That part of Virginia
called "West Virginia"
refused to secede
and was admitted
as a State in 1863.

ATLANTIC OCEAN

CUBA

GULF OF MEXICO

PACIFIC OCEAN

M E X I C O

MAINE
VT.
N.H.
MASS.
CONN. R.I.
NEW YORK
NEW JERSEY
PENNSYLVANIA
DEL.
M. D.
Washington
VIRGINIA
W. VA.
NORTH CAROLINA
SOUTH CAROLINA
OHIO
KENTUCKY
TENNESSEE
GEORGIA
ALABAMA
MISS.
FLORIDA
INDIANA
ILLINOIS
MICHIGAN
WISCONSIN
MINNESOTA
IOWA
MISSOURI
ARKANSAS
LOUISIANA
INDIAN TER.
KANSAS
TEXAS
NEBRASKA TER.
COLORADO TER.
NEW MEXICO TER.
DAKOTA TER.
WASHINGTON TER.
OREGON
NEVADA TER.
UTAH TER.
CALIFORNIA
PUBLIC LAND

Boston
New York
Buffalo
Philadelphia
Gettysburg
Cleveland
Cincinnati
Louisville
Perryville
Indianapolis
Chicago
Milwaukee
Detroit
St. Paul
Minneapolis
Des Moines
Kansas City
St. Louis
Wilsons Creek
Omaha
Denver
Colorado Springs
Santa Fe
Salt Lake City
Virginia City
Sacramento
San Francisco
Los Angeles
San Diego
Yuma
Portland
Astoria
Ft. Benton
Little Rock
Memphis
Corinth
Shiloh
Nashville
Bowling Green
Ft. Henry
Ft. Donelson
Chattanooga
Chickamauga
Resaca
Kennesaw Mtn.
Atlanta
Montgomery
Mobile
New Orleans
Vicksburg
Galveston
Austin
Jacksonville
Savannah
Beaufort
Ft. Sumter
Charleston
Columbia
Raleigh
Richmond
Appomattox C. H.
Fair Oaks
Seven Pines
Fredericksburg
Chancellorsville
Bull Run
Cedar Creek
Antietam
Norfolk
Hampton Roads
Harper's Ferry

St. Lawrence R.
Missouri R.
Yellowstone R.
Columbia R.
Snake R.
Colorado R.
Rio Grande
Red R.
Arkansas R.
Mississippi R.
Ohio R.

Congress passed a law prohibiting the bringing into the United States of more slaves. Smuggling was easy, however. In one year more than ten thousand Negro slaves were smuggled into New Orleans to be sold on the auction block to the highest bidder.

Many planters had a sense of personal responsibility toward their slaves, and sometimes an owner freed his slaves in his will. Yet it was often necessary to settle an estate by selling the slaves. By 1800 the slave trade was a big business, and was spreading to the Mississippi River. Overseers who came from the North as well as the South were often cruel and used the whip. To be "sold down the river" was a horrible threat to any slave, for conditions in New Orleans and west of the river were the worst in the South. In 1850 the price of slaves had risen. The *Wanderer* was the last slave ship to land a cargo of Africans in the United States.

It was difficult for a runaway slave to get to the free states in the North. The patrol was out everywhere. Slaves whispered, "The paterollers will get you if you don't look out!" And yet a few did make it on their own. After a while the famous Underground Railroad took over the job of smuggling slaves to freedom. Antislavery people in Illinois, Indiana, and Pennsylvania, as well as other northern states, made secret rooms behind closets in their homes. Slaves were passed on at night, riding under hay in wagons, to other homes. Way stations were secret, and were in an organized chain all the way to Canada. In defiance of the Fugitive Slave Laws, the system extended through fourteen states. After a time

the sea also became a link of the chain, and slaves were smuggled into New England ports by ship.

When the Civil War began the Underground Railroad had been used by at least seventy-five thousand slaves. It was organized in railroad terms, had two "presidents," and the routes were called "lines." The resting places were known as "stations." Slaves brought in by the Underground Railroad "conductors" were called "packages" or "freight."

The heroic Negro woman of the Underground Railroad was Harriet Tubman. She was a former slave and was known as "General Tubman" to her white friends. Slaves called her "Moses." She was a "conductor," making trips secretly into the South to lead fugitive Negroes north as Moses led his people into the Promised Land. Harriet Tubman was believed to have brought to freedom more than three hundred slaves.

In Kansas there was bloody fighting between slavery and antislavery people. A Negro named Dred Scott claimed his freedom because, with the consent of his master, he had lived in a free territory. The Supreme Court decided that a Negro was not a citizen and had no rights in law. The fury raised by this decision was one cause of the Civil War.

Those in the North who believed in the abolition of slavery were called abolitionists. Some of the best-known abolitionists between 1830 and 1861 were William Lloyd Garrison, Wendell Phillips, and a Quaker woman named Lucretia Mott. They and others wrote articles and pamphlets, and made speeches, and neither persecution nor riots could stop them. The martyr of the antislavery movement, who died in defense of freedom of speech and the press, was Elijah Lovejoy.

Born on a farm in Maine, Elijah grew up in a pious family. He became a Presbyterian minister and went to St. Louis, Missouri, to publish a religious newspaper. When he protested slavery and the sometimes brutal treatment of Negroes, his press was destroyed by a mob. Elijah Lovejoy made a famous statement on the freedom of the press given to all citizens by the Constitution of the United States.

When he was attacked again and his press silenced, he decided to move to Illinois, which was a free state. He ordered a new press, but soon found that there was as much violence in southern Illinois as in Missouri, for mobs destroyed his press once more. In 1837, Lovejoy and some friends received a new press and guarded it in a warehouse. In the night they were attacked, the building was set on fire, and Elijah Lovejoy was killed. Antislavery feeling boiled up all over the North when news came of the death of the antislavery journalist.

Lining up against each other in bitter feeling were Southerners with their plantations and slaves, and Northerners with their industrial cities. Harriet Beecher Stowe inflamed the country with her book, *Uncle Tom's Cabin* — and old John Brown, the wildest abolitionist of them all, was waging a one-man war of his own against slavery. As he gathered followers he moved from "Bleeding Kansas" to Canada, where he drew up a constitution and set up a government on paper. This old man with flowing white hair and beard had a dream of raising an army to liberate the slaves, and he believed that slaves would flock to it from all over the South.

Harpers Ferry, West Virginia, seemed to be a gateway to the South. It was also the site of a United States armory and arsenal. John Brown gathered his "army" of seventeen white men and five Negroes at Harpers Ferry. They would take the weapons and hold the arsenal! Slaves would flock to them in thousands. But John Brown's dream was only a dream after all, for no slaves came. The United States, instead, sent troops to lay siege to a fire engine house where John Brown and his men defended their cause. Soldiers, under the command of Colonel Robert E. Lee and Jeb Stuart, stormed the doors and captured the revolutionists.

John Brown and six of his followers were hanged at Charles Town on December 2, 1859. John Brown became a rallying name in the North for antislavery forces. In the South he was looked upon with contempt. The Civil War was closer!

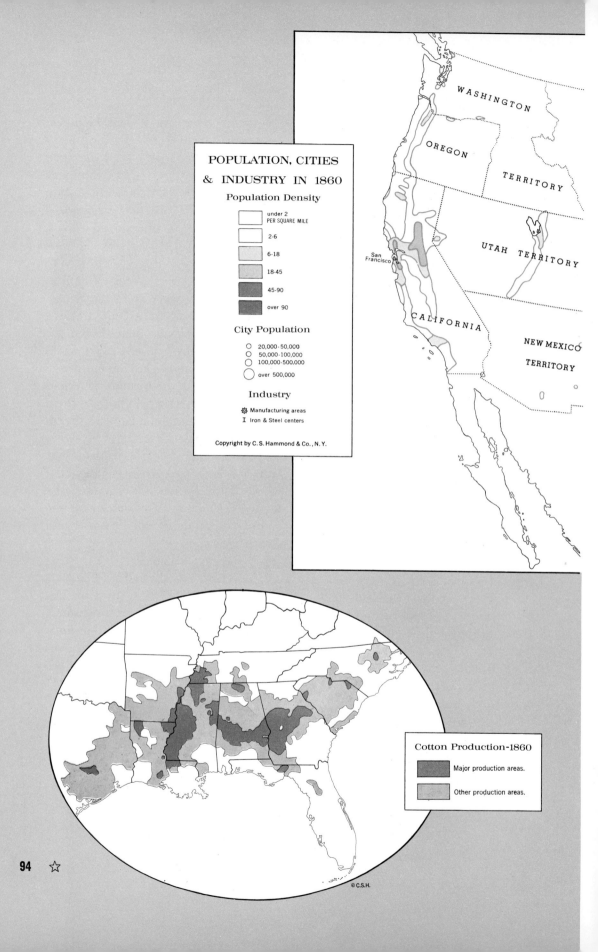

POPULATION, CITIES
& INDUSTRY IN 1860

Population Density

under 2
PER SQUARE MILE

2-6

6-18

18-45

45-90

over 90

City Population

○ 20,000-50,000
○ 50,000-100,000
○ 100,000-500,000
○ over 500,000

Industry

⚙ Manufacturing areas
I Iron & Steel centers

Copyright by C. S. Hammond & Co., N.Y.

WASHINGTON

OREGON

TERRITORY

San
Francisco

UTAH TERRITORY

CALIFORNIA

NEW MEXICO

TERRITORY

Cotton Production-1860

Major production areas.

Other production areas.

© C.S.H.

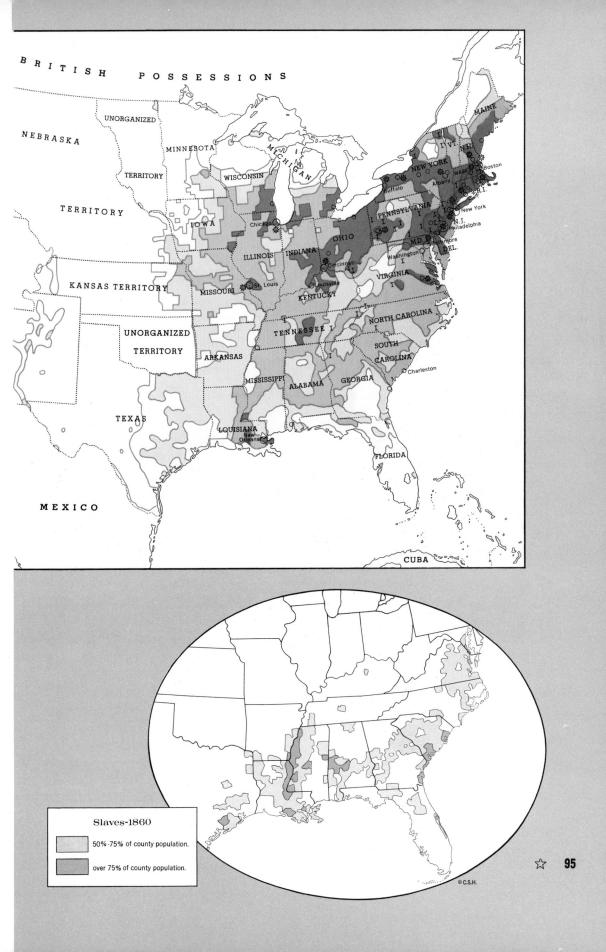

B R I T I S H   P O S S E S S I O N S

NEBRASKA

UNORGANIZED

MINNESOTA

TERRITORY

WISCONSIN

MICHIGAN

MAINE

VT.

N.H.

NEW YORK

Mass.

Boston

TERRITORY

Buffalo

Albany

R.I.

IOWA

Chicago

ILLINOIS

INDIANA

OHIO

PENNSYLVANIA

New York

Philadelphia

N.J.

MD.

Baltimore

DEL.

KANSAS TERRITORY

MISSOURI

St. Louis

Cincinnati

Louisville

Washington

KENTUCKY

VIRGINIA

NORTH CAROLINA

UNORGANIZED

TENNESSEE

TERRITORY

ARKANSAS

SOUTH
CAROLINA

MISSISSIPPI

ALABAMA

GEORGIA

Charleston

TEXAS

LOUISIANA

New
Orleans

FLORIDA

MEXICO

CUBA

Slaves-1860

50%-75% of county population.

over 75% of county population.

⭐ 95

©C.S.H.

MACHINES, MEN AND MOTION

17 In the northern and middle western free states rapid changes were taking place. New Orleans, the most important city of the South, was busy with slave trading, cotton, and sugar. By 1860 there were a million people in New York City. But St. Louis and Cincinnati, with their river trade, were mushrooming into the countryside. The 1850's saw the golden age of the merchant marine, of fast clipper ships and squareriggers, and of whaling vessels, with a rapid growth of coastal cities.

At a time when a few men were becoming millionaires, farmers worked hard for a small return. Yet they said, "I can stand on my own two feet and owe no man." Their sons were expected to do the same. Farmers found it hard to understand those boys who had restless feet and who often took off for the cities.

"If that old Commodore Vanderbilt and that immigrant fellow named Astor could get rich, well — so can I!"

John Jacob Astor, a butcher's son, arrived in New York in 1783. He brought with him a bundle containing a suit of Sunday clothes, seven flutes, and five pounds in money. Before long,

however, he was in the fur trade. He went out with a pack on his back to bring in valuable skins, paying the Indians for them with a jug of rum, or some beads, or cloth. By 1847 Astor was a financial king, with a huge trapping and trading empire extending from the Rockies to the Great Lakes. He owned ships — and was the richest man in America.

Cornelius Vanderbilt started with even less than did Astor. He could scarcely read or write, but he was full of energy and sharp of mind. He ferried passengers and freight from New York City to Staten Island. From one ferry boat he advanced to ownership of many ships, and soon was in the coasting trade. By now he was called "the Commodore." Vanderbilt paid low wages and drove out his competitors. He swept into his ownership huge railroad systems as well. Vanderbilt left a fortune to a family which grew richer in later generations. People marveled at this man who is said to have amassed a fortune of one million dollars in the space of fifteen years!

Inventions seldom made inventors rich, but they did enable some other people to become multimillionaires. A tiny locomotive called Tom Thumb, puffing along a narrow track in 1830, with a passenger coach bouncing along behind, ran its distance in 72 minutes. Few believed such a thing, except those who saw it with their own amazed cinder-filled eyes. Tom Thumb was the first locomotive built in America, and more soon followed. In the early half of the new century after the Revolution, America was bubbling with energy, new ideas, and inventions.

Robert Fulton was an engineer who was regarded as more than a little strange by his fellow citizens in New York City. In 1807 people ran to the waterfront to laugh and point at that small boat puffing steam, shaking, and rattling as Fulton and his partner, Robert Livingston, and their friends went on board for the first trip of the *Clermont* upriver to Albany.

"Look at the Toot! Just like a tea kettle," jeered the crowd. "She'll blow up. That's Fulton's Folly!"

Nevertheless, the little *Clermont* steamed slowly up the Hudson River, and back down again — and steam navigation had been launched in the United States. The era of river boats began. Whistles blew, boilers were stoked with wood, and later with coal, and paddle wheels churned the waters. On the seas wooden ships, with their clouds of sails, gave way to iron hulls and engines. Propellers took the place of paddles on inland waters. Robert Fulton continued inventing, and made machines for spinning flax for linen, for twisting fiber into rope, and for sawing and polishing marble.

After the War of Independence, in 1789, Samuel Slater came from England to America. President Andrew Jackson called Slater "the Father of American Manufactures," because he built the nation's first factory. It was a cotton mill in Rhode Island. Twenty years after that there were about 165 such mills in the United States. Eli Whitney invented the cotton gin in 1793, then turned his inventive mind to firearms and opened a factory in Connecticut for making muskets.

The sewing machine! That started factories and brought women into them. Vulcanization of rubber — commercial petroleum — textiles — food processing — improvement in tools! And how many others! Industry drew men to the cities in the 1850's. Twenty years earlier the reaper invented by Cyrus McCormick, who had a farm of his own, enabled him to put up a small factory in a swampy little frontier town called Chicago. Before that time wheat had been imported from Europe. Soon ships were taking American grain to ports around the world, and Chicago was the meatpacking center of America.

Then Sam Colt, who had liked fireworks so much as a boy that he had blown the windows out of his school, invented the Colt revolver. Texas Rangers ordered a large supply. It was an inventor, also known as a famous artist, who devised the "lightning wire," or telegraph, and sent the first message. Samuel Morse tapped out, "What hath God wrought?"

While inventions were coming thick and fast, and industries growing in cities and towns, workmen found themselves in a sad situation. They had to labor day and night, and often for such low wages that their families found it necessary to work in the factories, also.

☆ 97

As early as 1792 shoemakers in Philadelphia had joined together to protect themselves. Two years later typesetters founded the Typographical Society in New York. Workmen wanted higher wages and better places to work and to live, as well as shorter hours. Employers' organizations, formed to serve the owners and protect their rights, followed. Trade unions grew in number, and strikes and layoffs began.

New ideas of all kinds were taking root in this nineteenth century. Art, literature, music, and reforms were blossoming. Some ideas were so new that they frightened people. In the educational field such thinkers as Henry Barnard, Horace Mann, Emma Willard and Mary Lyon were called "dangerous radicals" because they wanted to tax all property owners to educate all children. But the educators kept on saying, "Every schoolhouse that is opened closes a jail."

In 1841 a young woman set out to discover conditions in jails and insane asylums. Dorothea Dix found that the insane were often placed in prisons and treated worse than hardened criminals. They were chained to walls in cellars, as well as starved and beaten. She walked quietly through prisons and poorhouses, and her eyes did not miss much. When she wrote about these places people were horrified. Laws were passed to improve prisons and hospitals. Miss Dix traveled as far west as Illinois, and to Louisiana in the South. By the time that she was ready to leave a city, citizens were already making plans to improve their jails and mental institutions.

Southerners called poor workers of the North in slums and sweatshops the "real slaves," while many citizens in the North felt that underpaid and overworked people were better off than the Negro slaves. In the year 1861, as Abraham Lincoln became President, there were two questions that were about to split the nation. Could the United States of America permit slavery? And could a state secede from the Union?

South Carolina answered the second question on December 20, 1860 by withdrawing from the Union. On March 4, 1861 cannon roared a salute to the new President of the United States. Abraham Lincoln, born in the South — backwoodsman, lawyer, Congressman, President — believed that the Nation was "one and indivisible." There could no longer be any compromise on the question of slavery. Then six other Southern states seceded, and Jefferson Davis became President of the Confederate States of America.

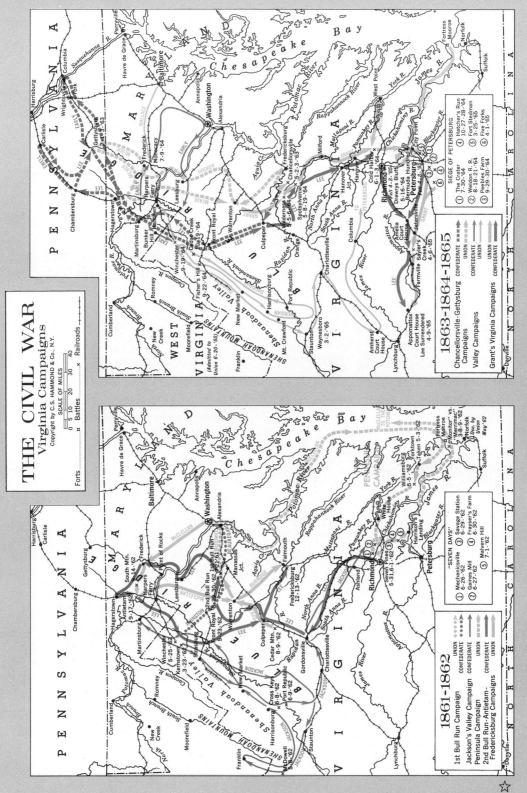

THE CIVIL WAR
Virginia Campaigns
Copyright by C.S. Hammond & Co., N.Y.

SCALE OF MILES

0 5 10 20 30 40

Forts .... □ Battles .... × Railroads ——+——

1863–1864–1865

Chancellorsville–Gettysburg Campaigns

Valley Campaigns

Grant's Virginia Campaigns

SIEGE OF PETERSBURG

① The Crater 7-30-'64
② Weldon R. R. 8-18-21-'64
③ Peebles Farm 9-29-30-'64
④ Hatcher's Run 10-27-28-'64
⑤ Fort Stedman 3-25-'65
⑥ Five Forks 4-1-'65

1861–1862

1st Bull Run Campaign

Jackson's Valley Campaign

Peninsula Campaign

2nd Bull Run–Antietam–Fredericksburg Campaigns

UNION
CONFEDERATE
CONFEDERATE
UNION
CONFEDERATE
UNION

"SEVEN DAYS"

① Mechanicsville 6-26-'62
② Gaines Mill 6-27-'62
③ Savage Station 6-29-'62
④ Frayser's Farm 6-30-'62
⑤ Malvern Hill 7-1-'62

OUR NATION DIVIDES

18

"We'll hang John Brown to a sour apple tree," shouted Southerners.

"We'll hang Jeff Davis to a sour apple tree," sang Northerners.

In the harbor of Charleston, South Carolina, a handful of Union troops were under siege by Confederates. Jefferson Davis demanded that they leave. Abraham Lincoln ordered them to remain in Fort Sumter. The President of the United States sent ships with provisions to the federal fort. At four-thirty in the morning of April 12, 1861, Citadel Square, in Charleston, glowed with swinging lanterns. Streets rang with the sound of marching soldiers, cavalry horses, and rolling drums. A command was given on shore, "Fire!" A Confederate shell struck Fort Sumter. The Civil War had begun.

General Robert E. Lee, a Virginian and the most distinguished officer in the army, was asked to lead the Union army. He chose to remain with the South. Some of his Confederate officers were Stonewall Jackson, P. G. T. Beauregard, Jeb Stuart, and the two Johnstons, Albert Sidney and Joseph E. Opposing him were other friends, Ulysses S. Grant, W. T. Sherman,

George Meade, and Winfield Scott, old warrior of the War of 1812 and the Mexican War.

Southerners were in a state of wild excitement. Men rode off to join the Confederate forces, while their ladies waved good-bye. In the North recruits came to Washington to enlist. Mrs. Julia Ward Howe heard regiments marching and gun carriages rattling past her windows as she wrote the most famous song of the conflict,

"Mine eyes have seen the glory of the coming of the Lord,

He is trampling out the vintage where the grapes of wrath are stored . . ."

North and South there was a picnic spirit. In Washington men in army blue were drilling. So were militiamen in crimson Zouave dress, or Scottish kilts. Regiments of citizens in city suits and straw hats wheeled and turned and presented arms. "One, two, three — Hup!" Some of the militia wore Italian and French uniforms. There were groups of big lumberjacks down from the backwoods, with knives and horse pistols thrust in their belts.

Below the Mason-Dixon Line some

of the same sort of dress showed up, although army uniforms were gray. There were also back country volunteers in homespun butternut jeans alongside fancy militia uniforms, with their plumes and sashes. On both sides everyone took it for granted that the war would be won quickly.

Washington society turned out in carriages and on horses to watch the first battle of Manassas, or Bull Run. They expected victory — instead, they saw Union troops routed. In a wild panic the holiday crowd fled back to the city. After that day Lincoln and his government got down to planning for a long war. Later the Confederate army plunged up from Richmond into Pennsylvania, and came to the very edge of Washington. "Rebels" also moved west to the Shenandoah Valley.

While Union forces had the advantage of superiority in supplies of men, arms and materials, the Confederate army had great leadership in the Army of Northern Virginia. At the start, General McClellan pushed down almost to Richmond, Virginia, and was then forced to retreat. General Lee advanced into Maryland. In a bloody battle at Antietam Lee, with forty thousand men, held off McClellan who had eighty thousand in his attacking strength. Just as it looked hopeless for the Confederates, reinforcements arrived, and McClellan's Federal line retreated. Lincoln removed General McClellan from command. Lee withdrew his army into Virginia. The Federal Army of the Potomac, now under General Pope, was defeated at a second battle of Bull Run, at Fredericksburg, and again at Chancellorsville. Yet there Lee suffered a great loss, for General Stonewall Jackson was accidentally killed by one of his own men.

There had been wars before, but none like this in America. Sometimes it was father against son, brother against brother, and friend against friend. Billy Yank yelled, "Hoo-RAY!" as he charged the enemy. Johnny Reb gave out his rebel yell — called half war whoop and half wolf howl. "Wo-who-EEEY!" Both sides fought valiantly. On both sides troops lived on food that was often only hardtack biscuit and salt-horse pork. They had almost no medical care, not enough supplies, and often not even tents. Yet they joked and sang a great deal.

"Just before the battle the general heard a row. He says the Yanks are coming, I can hear their rifles now. He turns around in wonder, and what do you think he sees? The Georgia militia eating goober peas!"

"Tramp, tramp, tramp the boys are marching . . ."

Enemies were friendly across the lines between battles. Men swapped tobacco and food, yelled good-natured taunts, and pickets often leaned on their muskets to talk back and forth. From time to time boys in blue and gray even sang together, in a strange concert. They admired each other's courage and pitied each other's suffering. During the second Battle of Bull Run two Confederates carrying a wounded comrade heard a Yankee challenge, followed by, "You're inside Union lines. Go back and turn to your right." "You've got a heart in you," called out Johnny Reb.

Both armies had drummer boys. Nine-year-old Johnny Clem ran away to join the Twenty-second Michigan

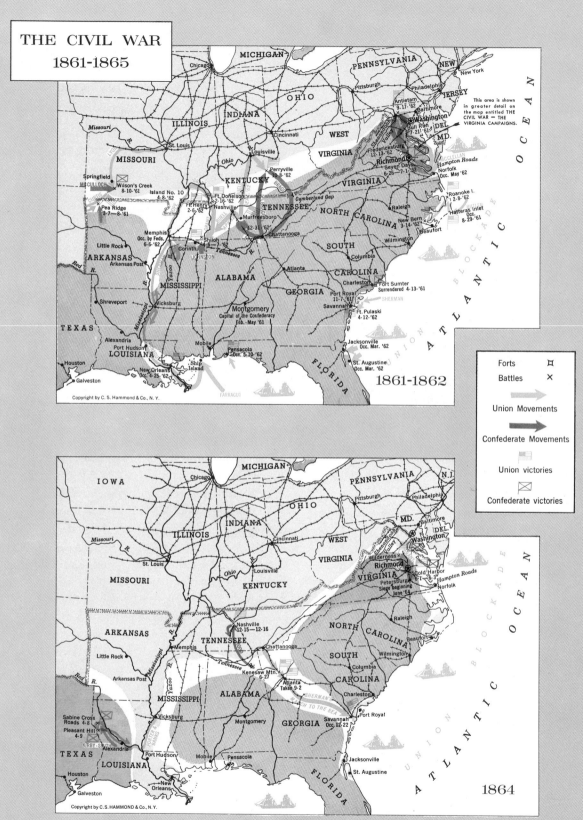

THE CIVIL WAR
1861-1865

1861-1862

MICHIGAN
Chicago
PENNSYLVANIA
NEW
New York
OHIO
Pittsburgh
Philadelphia
JERSEY
ILLINOIS
INDIANA
Antietam
9-17-'62
Baltimore
Washington
DEL.
Cincinnati
WEST
Bull Run
7-21-'61
MD.
This area is shown in greater detail on the map entitled THE CIVIL WAR — THE VIRGINIA CAMPAIGNS.
Missouri
St. Louis
Louisville
VIRGINIA
Fredericksburg
12-13-'62
Ohio
MISSOURI
Richmond
MCCLELLAN
Hampton Roads
Norfolk
Occ. May '62
Springfield
MCCULLOCH
Perryville
10-8-'62
KENTUCKY
Seven Days
6-26-7-1-'62
Wilson's Creek
8-10-'61
Island No. 10
4-8-'62
VIRGINIA
Roanoke I.
1-2-8-'62
Pea Ridge
3-7-8-'61
Ft. Donelson
2-16-'62
Ft. Henry
2-6-'62
Nashville
Cumberland Gap
Raleigh
NORTH
New Bern
3-14-'62
Hatteras Inlet
Occ.
8-29-'61
TENNESSEE
CAROLINA
Murfreesboro
12-31-'62
Wilmington
Beaufort
Memphis
Occ. by Feds.
6-6-'62
Shiloh
4-6-7-'62
Chattanooga
SOUTH
Little Rock
Corinth
JOHNSTON
Columbia
ARKANSAS
Tennessee
CAROLINA
Arkansas Post
Atlanta
Charleston
Fort Sumter
Surrendered 4-13-'61
MISSISSIPPI
ALABAMA
GEORGIA
Port Royal
11-7-'61
SHERMAN
Shreveport
Vicksburg
Savannah
Ft. Pulaski
4-12-'62
Montgomery
Capital of the Confederacy
Feb.-May '61
TEXAS
Alexandria
Port Hudson
LOUISIANA
Mobile
Pensacola
Occ. 5-10-'62
Jacksonville
Occ. Mar. '62
Houston
Ship
Island
St. Augustine
Occ. Mar. '62
Galveston
New Orleans
Occ. 4-25-'62
FLORIDA
FARRAGUT
Copyright by C. S. Hammond & Co., N. Y.
1861-1862

ATLANTIC OCEAN
UNION BLOCKADE

Forts ⌗
Battles ✕
Union Movements
Confederate Movements
Union victories
Confederate victories

1864

IOWA
MICHIGAN
Chicago
PENNSYLVANIA
N.J.
OHIO
Pittsburgh
Philadelphia
ILLINOIS
INDIANA
Cincinnati
WEST
MD.
Baltimore
DEL.
Washington
Missouri
St. Louis
VIRGINIA
Wilderness
Richmond
Cold Harbor
6-1-'3
Hampton Roads
MISSOURI
Ohio
Louisville
KENTUCKY
VIRGINIA
Petersburg
Siege beginning
June '64
Norfolk
Raleigh
ARKANSAS
Nashville
12-15-12-16
NORTH CAROLINA
Little Rock
Memphis
TENNESSEE
Chattanooga
Wilmington
Beaufort
Kenesaw Mtn.
6-27
SOUTH
Columbia
Arkansas Post
Kenesaw Mtn.
Atlanta
Taken 9-2
CAROLINA
Charleston
SHERMAN'S MARCH TO THE SEA
MISSISSIPPI
ALABAMA
Sabine Cross
Roads 4-8
Vicksburg
Montgomery
GEORGIA
Port Royal
Pleasant Hill
4-9
Savannah
Occ. 12-22
KIRBY-SMITH
PORTER & BANKS
Alexandria
TEXAS
Port Hudson
Mobile
Pensacola
Jacksonville
LOUISIANA
Houston
St. Augustine
Galveston
New Orleans
FLORIDA
Copyright by C. S. HAMMOND & Co., N. Y.
1864

ATLANTIC OCEAN
UNION BLOCKADE

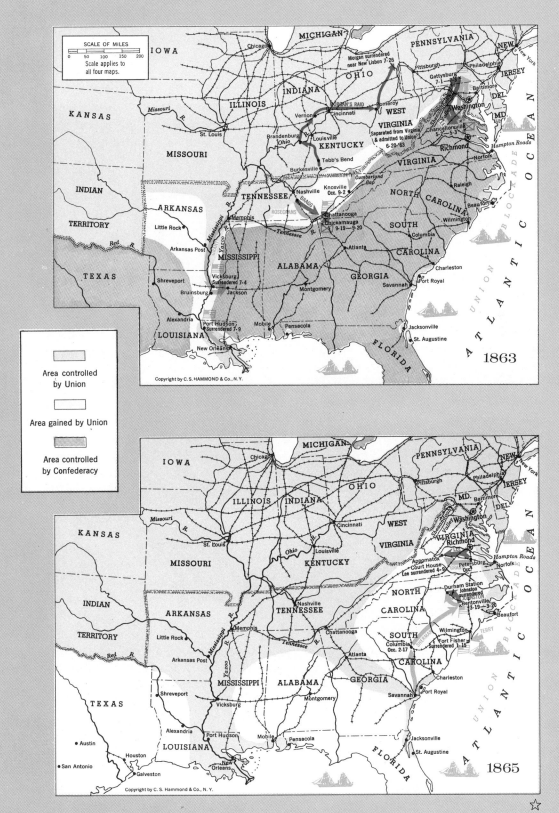

SCALE OF MILES
0 50 100 150 200
Scale applies to
all four maps.

Area controlled
by Union

Area gained by Union

Area controlled
by Confederacy

1863

IOWA
MICHIGAN
PENNSYLVANIA
NEW
Chicago
Morgan surrendered
near New Lisbon 7-26
Pittsburgh
Philadelphia
JERSEY
OHIO
Gettysburg
7-1
New York
KANSAS
INDIANA
Baltimore
DEL.
ILLINOIS
MORGAN'S RAID
Pomeroy
WEST
Washington
MD.
Missouri R.
Vernon
Cincinnati
St. Louis
Brandenburg
Ohio
Louisville
VIRGINIA
Separated from Virginia
& admitted to Union
6-20-'63
Chancellorsville
5-2 5-3
MISSOURI
KENTUCKY
Richmond
Norfolk
Tebb's Bend
Hampton Roads
Burkesville
VIRGINIA
Raleigh
Cumberland
Gap
Knoxville
Occ. 9-2
NORTH CAROLINA
INDIAN
ARKANSAS
TENNESSEE
Nashville
BRAGG
Beaufort
Little Rock
Memphis
ROSECRANS
Chattanooga
SOUTH
Wilmington
TERRITORY
Tennessee R.
Chickamauga
9-19 9-20
Columbia
Red R.
Arkansas Post
Atlanta
CAROLINA
TEXAS
MISSISSIPPI
ALABAMA
Charleston
Vicksburg
Surrendered 7-4
GEORGIA
Shreveport
Jackson
Savannah
Port Royal
Bruinsburg
Montgomery
Alexandria
Port Hudson
Surrendered 7-9
Mobile
Pensacola
LOUISIANA
Jacksonville
New Orleans
St. Augustine
FLORIDA
ATLANTIC OCEAN
UNION BLOCKADE
Copyright by C.S. HAMMOND & Co., N.Y.

1865

IOWA
MICHIGAN
PENNSYLVANIA
NEW
Chicago
Pittsburgh
Philadelphia
JERSEY
OHIO
New York
MD.
Baltimore
ILLINOIS
INDIANA
DEL.
Cincinnati
WEST
Washington
Missouri R.
VIRGINIA
Richmond
St. Louis
Ohio R.
Louisville
VIRGINIA
Appomatox
Court House
Lee surrendered 4-9
Petersburg
Occ.
Hampton Roads
Norfolk
KANSAS
MISSOURI
KENTUCKY
GRANT
Durham Station
Johnston
surrendered
INDIAN
Nashville
Bentonville
3-19 3-20
Beaufort
ARKANSAS
TENNESSEE
NORTH
CAROLINA
Little Rock
Memphis
Chattanooga
TERRITORY
Tennessee R.
Wilmington
TERRY
Arkansas Post
Atlanta
SOUTH
Columbia
Occ. 2-17
Fort Fisher
Surrendered 1-15
Red R.
Yazoo R.
SHERMAN
CAROLINA
Shreveport
MISSISSIPPI
ALABAMA
GEORGIA
Charleston
Vicksburg
Alexandria
Montgomery
Savannah
Port Royal
TEXAS
Austin
Port Hudson
Mobile
Pensacola
Houston
LOUISIANA
Jacksonville
San Antonio
New
Orleans
St. Augustine
Galveston
FLORIDA
ATLANTIC OCEAN
UNION BLOCKADE
Copyright by C.S. Hammond & Co., N.Y.

Regiment. After a shell smashed his drum they called him Johnny Shiloh. Then he took up a cut-down musket because he wanted to shoot back. At Chickamauga he rode an artillery carriage into battle. At twelve he was made a sergeant and some ladies in Chicago sewed him a uniform. At the Battle of Atlanta, in 1864, he was wounded and his pony shot down under him. He lived to become an officer in the regular army.

Eddie Evans, drummer boy of the Twenty-fourth Mississippi, marched out in front of his regiment and stood only fifty yards from the Yankee lines during the fighting at Atlanta. He waved a flag and rallied the Confederate troops to their cause. Cadets from military schools in the South were as brave and daring as seasoned soldiers. They went into battles in all of the campaigns.

In July, 1863, the Battle of Gettysburg was fought. On the third day of intense fighting the two armies faced each other from hillsides. Led by General G. E. Pickett Confederates charged across golden wheat fields in a deadly artillery fire. They fell, rose, and charged again. They could not take the hill. Pickett's Charge, so brave and so tragic, marked a change in the tide of the war. President Lincoln, pacing his rooms in the night, began to hope for victory soon. Lee's troops retreated into Virginia. Both armies went into winter quarters but, although Union soldiers were getting more supplies, Confederates remained hungry and ragged.

The Mississippi Campaign was begun at St. Louis, Missouri, by General Grant, who faced 80 miles of strong Confederate fortifications. Grant attacked and captured the first line of defense by taking two forts, and led his army to Shiloh, where he almost lost the battle, but finally forced General Albert Sidney Johnston to pull back. The Vicksburg siege ended a brave and desperate defense after forty-seven days. General Grant now had the Confederacy split into two parts. He sent General William Tecumseh Sherman on his terrible march to the sea. The Battle of Atlanta saw a valiant defense by Confederate troops who were badly overpowered in men and in weapons. As Sherman's victorious army advanced it left the city of Atlanta in flames. Sherman's army cut a wide swath through a Georgia already hungry and desolated by more than three years of war. His fighting men were followed by a riffraff of "foragers" or "bummers," who were allowed to steal anything they wanted, and who had orders to burn and destroy everything left behind. At Savannah, on the sea, Sherman sent word to Lincoln that he gave him Georgia as a Christmas present.

At Appomattox General Lee surrendered to General Grant. The Confederate leader mounted his horse, Traveller, to say farewell to his army. Union troops stood in silence, their officers saluting Lee by raising their hats. Southern soldiers gave up their weapons and bloodstained regimental colors. It was April 9, 1865. Five nights later President Lincoln was shot down in Ford's Theater by a crazed actor, John Wilkes Booth. When Abraham Lincoln died he left a country that was now without a strong and compassionate spirit to guide it.

THE RAILS POINT WEST

In Texas, before the Civil War, people had shouted, "Remember the Alamo!" In the California gold rush it was "Pike's Peak or Bust!" and on the way back sometimes, "Pike's Peak and Busted!" The Mormon saying, on reaching Utah, was, "All is well." And Horace Greeley, the journalist, started off many with his, "Go west, young man!"

Then came the long rails and the Iron Horse. Railroads had run for a long time in the East, and before that in England, where James Watt had invented the steam engine. However, locomotives were risky things. They blew up. Their wooden trestles fell down. They hit cows and sent horses to running away. In summer railway cars were roasting hot, blacking the faces of riders with soot. In winter they stalled in snowdrifts and their pot-bellied stoves set the cars on fire. Train travel was more dangerous than wild horses, or rocking stagecoaches with a man riding shotgun, eye peeled for bandits. Yet railroads doggedly pushed onto plains and up into mountains, and people crowded into the cars! There were so many head-on collisions that songs were sung about them.

"Casey Jones! Two locomotives! Casey Jones! That's a-going to bump!"

Railroads, thrusting into the wild west played a big part in taming it. They helped bring U.S. marshals, law courts, fire engines, schools, and churches. They created rail towns for cattle shipment. Herds of longhorns were driven by cowhands along the Chisholm Trail from Texas to Abilene, Kansas, to be loaded for the Chicago stockyards. Trail riders pushed their bawling cows on the long, dusty Western Cattle Trail to Dodge City, Kansas. "Whoopitee-i-o, get along little dogie. It's your misfortune and none of my own."

Railroads shoved into towns where the Earp brothers, Bat Masterson, and Wild Bill Hickock were no faster with the shooting iron than such ladies as Annie Oakley, Belle Starr and Calamity Jane.

After the end of the Civil War the government gave railroad companies vast tracts of land. Resentful settlers were told that these land grants opened up the country and brought in wealth. Land was given in alternate sections of

19

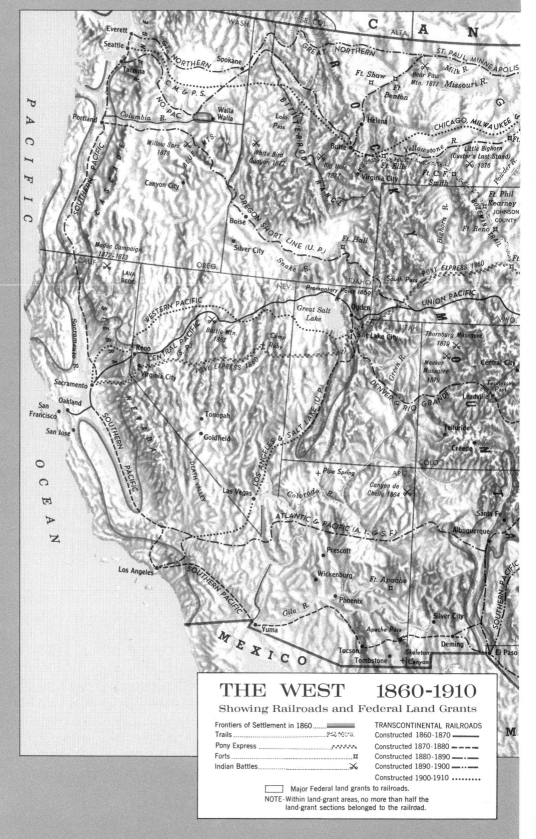

THE WEST 1860-1910

Showing Railroads and Federal Land Grants

Frontiers of Settlement in 1860 ....

Trails ....

Pony Express ....

Forts ....

Indian Battles ....

TRANSCONTINENTAL RAILROADS

Constructed 1860-1870

Constructed 1870-1880 — — —

Constructed 1880-1890 — · —

Constructed 1890-1900 — ·· —

Constructed 1900-1910 ········

Major Federal land grants to railroads.

NOTE—Within land-grant areas, no more than half the
land-grant sections belonged to the railroad.

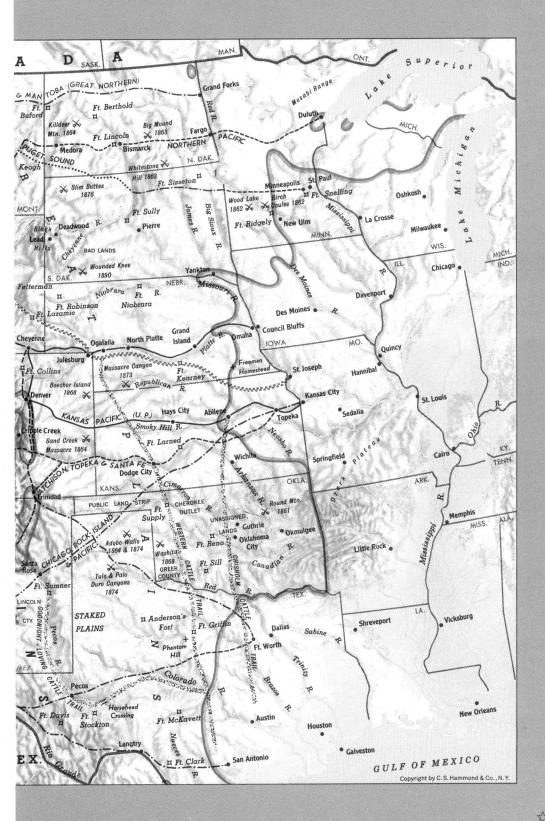

six to twenty miles on either side of the tracks, with government-owned sections in between, making a checkerboard pattern. In return railroads carried mails, government freight, and troops at a reduced rate. This caused some of the western settlers, who were hostile to the railroad, to feel more sympathy for train robbers than they should have felt.

And yet the long, lonesome voice of the train whistle was a welcome sound on a prairie farm. To some it was the sound of life passing swiftly, yet full of excitement. It meant the arrival of goods — maybe even a piano, or a printing press. To a gaily dressed crowd it sounded for a happy day's excursion or a Fourth of July picnic.

On July 10, 1865, the first spike of the new Transcontinental Railroad was driven into the earth in Omaha, Nebraska. Several thousand men joined the work gangs laying track for the Union Pacific. They were mainly Irish immigrants, but there were also ex-soldiers from both the Confederate and Union armies, along with mule skinners and former miners. "Drill ye tarriers, drill," sang the Irish as they pounded rail, pointing west. On the newly laid tracks, as fast as they went down, came locomotives hauling cars filled with supplies. Shack towns followed immediately along the right of way. Indians, watching on their horses at a distance, did not like this invasion of their buffalo country. There were frequent attacks when war parties swept down on track layers, who were forced to keep rifles and revolvers close by them as they worked. All the way across Nebraska and Wyoming graders and tracklayers defended themselves against Sioux and Cheyenne. Some army troops accompanied the work crews, but there weren't enough for any real protection.

There was one day when a band of Sioux braves rode down on a few workmen, who leaped onto a railroad handcar and pumped their way to safety just ahead of the Indians on their fast ponies. Yet the tracks advanced across plains and into mountains, toward a point at which the westbound Union Pacific expected to meet the eastward moving Central Pacific.

Railroad building from California was a tough struggle against severe winter storms and difficult mountains. When Charles Crocker recruited Chinese laborers to dig and grade the line for the Central Pacific people thought him crazy. Chinese were small men, not known for muscle, and unused to extreme cold. And yet four thousand of them joined the railroad gangs, and turned out to be excellent workmen. These little men in blue clothing with pigtails swinging under straw hats helped drill the Summit Tunnel, high in the Sierra Mountains, through solid rock.

The railroad kept moving forward, rails laid, trains following to end of track, and then on again. Through blizzards Chinese gangs pushed forward, six thousand feet up in the mountain range, with snowplows constantly clearing the way, and with avalanches sometimes burying men and camps. Indians were not a serious problem to the Central Pacific line, because passes for passenger cars were given to chiefs of the Paiute and Shoshoni tribes, and Indians were allowed to ride free on freight cars whenever they wished. By

1868 both railroads were in a race, trying to outdo each other in laying track, with Chinese and Irish working at increasing speed.

Construction crews from east and west met at Promontory Point, Utah, May 10, 1869. The Central Pacific was built by four men, Leland Stanford, Collis P. Huntington, Charles Crocker, and Mark Hopkins, who had in twenty years became millionaires in California. Leland Stanford, president of the line, drove in a golden spike, while a crowd watched and cheered. The whole nation rejoiced. Guns boomed and speeches were made — north, south, east, and west. America — ocean to ocean! In Washington a golden ball descended from a pole by magnetic impulse sent out from Promontory Point itself!

Railroad lines spread rapidly over the west. Some were locals, on tiny narrow gauge three-foot track. Others were transcontinental trains. In Colorado a railroad war was fought between the Denver and Rio Grande, and the Atchison, Topeka and Santa Fe. Both railroads went to court, and both sent out armed men to hold passes claimed by each. Bat Masterson, marshal of Dodge City, was hired by the Santa Fe Railroad to defend its roundhouse in Pueblo, Colorado. There were beatings and shootings until the Supreme Court decided in favor of the Denver and Rio Grande.

In stagecoach days Wells Fargo was the express company most often held up by bandits. Then holdup men began to rob trains, terrorizing and stealing from passengers, just as they took Wells Fargo treasure boxes. The most famous bank and train robber was Jesse James. Many holdup men, such as the James, Daltons, and Youngers were cold-blooded murderers, and not Robin Hoods as legend sometimes describes them. After Jesse James was killed a popular ballad was written, turning him into a hero.

As locomotives sped across grassy plains passengers leaned from windows to shoot confused, frightened buffalo for sport. Hides were valuable, and the beasts were also slain by commercial hunters until the huge herds were no more. Starving Indians mourned, and asked, "Where have the herds gone? When will they come again?"

Railway depots were crowded with trappers, frontiersmen in buckskin, eastern businessmen, peddlers, and soldiers. Everybody in town ran to see the railway cars come puffing in. Fred Harvey was a boy when he came from England to America in 1876. Some years later, as he traveled, he found western depot food to be unappetizing, and this gave him an idea. He started a chain of restaurants on the Santa Fe Railway. Travelers could not believe their eyes when they saw linen tablecloths, silver, and good food. They were overcome at sight of the Harvey girls —those nice, pretty girls from the East! These waitresses were so attractive that most of them married railroad men. Soon, in little towns along the railway lines, there was a large crop of babies named Fred or Harvey, for the immigrant lad who had come to America to make his fortune.

England, Scotland & Wales

British migration was dominant in the colonial period of American history. In the nineteenth and twentieth centuries, British migrants were sizeable elements in the population of the urban East and the Rocky Mountain area.

Ireland

The Irish, a major group since the potato famine of the 1840's, have concentrated largely in the New England and Middle Atlantic states.

Germany

In the last one hundred years Germany has sent more immigrants to the United States than any other nation. German migrants were represented strongly in most states outside of the South in 1910.

PATTERNS
OF NATIONALITIES

Showing Distribution of Foreign Born

PERCENT OF POPULATION OF EACH STATE BORN IN PRINCIPAL FOREIGN COUNTRIES ACCORDING TO CENSUS OF 1910

- less than 1%
- 1% to 2%
- 2% to 3%
- 3% to 4%
- 4% to 5%
- 5% to 6%
- 6% and over

Immigration to the United States in the nineteenth century was largely made up of Western European peoples—Germans, Irish, Swedes, English, etc. In the twentieth century the largest number of immigrants came from Southern and Eastern Europe — Italians, Poles and natives of the Russian and Austro-Hungarian Empires. Therefore, the year 1910 has been chosen as a base year for these maps because at that time both groups were present in sufficient numbers to be statistically significant.

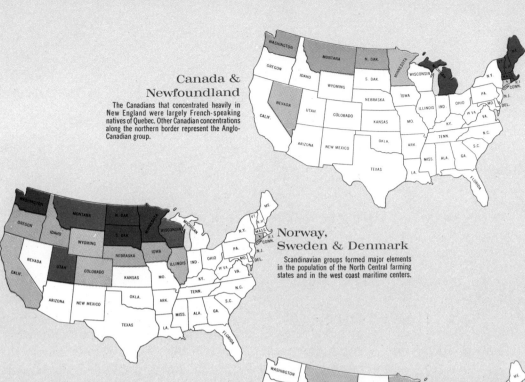

Canada & Newfoundland

The Canadians that concentrated heavily in New England were largely French-speaking natives of Quebec. Other Canadian concentrations along the northern border represent the Anglo-Canadian group.

Norway, Sweden & Denmark

Scandinavian groups formed major elements in the population of the North Central farming states and in the west coast maritime centers.

Austro-Hungarian Monarchy

Immigrants from the Austro-Hungarian Monarchy were largely drawn from the Slavic peoples of that dominion Czechs, Slovaks, Poles from Galicia, Croats and Slovenes.

Russian Empire

Immigrants from the Russian Empire were largely non-Russian minority groups such as Jews, Poles, Lithuanians, etc. The Jewish people were an especially large part of this migration and have concentrated heavily in New York City.

Italy

Italians arrived in great numbers after 1900. The majority have concentrated in the urban centers of the Northeast.

NEW CITIZENS FROM OLD LANDS

20 Since 1820 more than forty million people have come to America! They poured from ships' gangplanks into ports on the Atlantic and Pacific Oceans. They came to cities and towns on the Gulf of Mexico. They arrived overland from Mexico and Canada. Only the aborigines, misnamed Indians, were here when white men came. Most of the immigrants were from the British Isles and Europe. Until 1924, when the stream of new arrivals was slowed to a trickle by the Immigration Act, all of those who wanted to find a better life, and had the energy, and money for a ticket, could come. American railroads sent abroad booklets with pictures and rosy descriptions of the Promised Land. Golden opportunities on easy terms! Come one — come all!

Westward sailed the English, Scottish, and Welsh in Colonial times. There were Swedish and Dutch also, but most colonists came from the British Isles in the early days. Before 1883, eighty-five percent came from the northern and western European countries. After that time most of the foreign-born coming into Boston, Philadelphia, and New York were from the southern and eastern countries of Europe. Irish people were starving in the wake of the great potato famine in the 1840's, and a flood of Irish farmers crossed the Atlantic Ocean. More than a million Irish men and women came to America and Canada at that time. Those who could, sent money back to bring relatives over from the old country. Most of the Irish who came were without education or labor skills. In the time of Washington and Jefferson they worked on the National Road through Pennsylvania. They built canals, and then railroads. Like other foreign-born laborers, with education many of the Irish rose to prosperity. By 1920, there were more people of Irish ancestry in the United States than in Ireland.

After the Civil War Germans arrived in such numbers that their language was heard all over the country. Some came to escape military service. Russians, Italians, Austrians, Hungarians! They appeared in a riot of bright peasant costumes and with many different languages. At first they were shuttled into Castle Garden Immigration Station. This building, on a tiny island close to the shore of New York City, in a setting of sailboats and steamers, had once been a fine theater. There Jenny Lind, the Swedish Nightingale, had sung in 1850. After 1892 Ellis Island, in the harbor, received the flood of foreign-born and Castle Garden became an aquarium.

Before laws refused entrance to most immigrants and Ellis Island was abandoned in 1954, more than fifteen million people had landed there. They carried carpetbags and sacks stuffed with clothing and their few precious belongings. Irishmen wore steeple hats, Scots strode ashore in tartan kilts, Italians came in dark suits and caps of many kinds. Dutchmen took up extra room in line with their broad shoulders and wide pantaloons. Greeks, Bohemians, Russians, Germans, and Hungarians made a jangle of language that echoed against the bare walls of the buildings of Ellis Island.

Babies were born there, too. Some of the old folks, coming so far, died before the end of their journey. Yet these people had all seen, as their ships came into harbor, the Statue of Liberty holding aloft her torch and her book. They could not read the poem, written by Emma Lazarus, and inscribed on the base of the statue. Yet, somehow, they knew the meaning of it. It ended with the lines,

"Send these, the homeless, tempest-
    tossed to me,
I lift my lamp beside the golden
    door!"

At Ellis Island men waited with railroad tickets for sale. Many immigrants were taken to New Jersey and put into zulu cars on trains, and never even saw the city on Manhattan Island. In the early years most of those who took the zulu cars for immigrants were Germans going into the northwest to homestead farms. Then cars were jammed with families from many nations, and railroading boomed with the crowds. Zulu cars were built with rough sleeping bunks; some were set aside for women and children, and others for men. People of the same nationalities clung together, and all had baskets filled with food for the journey. A zulu car was noisy with talk and with crying children, as well as with the mewing of pet cats and barking of dogs. It was thick with the scent of smoked fish, sausage, bread, and cheese. It was both lively and sad with old world song. Zithers and concertinas, violins and Jew's harps brought laughter and tears, drawing forth memories of their lost homes. Yet always, as the wheels rolled westward, they kept their hopeful eyes on "The Land of Milk and Honey."

Thousands of workingmen and women were needed in Chicago, New York, Boston, Philadelphia, and other cities and towns in the east and midwest. Immigrant trains carried them to these places. Many Irishmen became policemen, hodcarriers, or went into business, and both Irish and Scandinavian women became domestic servants. Industry of all kinds grew so rapidly that it mushroomed to huge size, and demanded a great deal of labor.

Cornishmen and Welshmen, who had been miners in the British Isles, went to work in the coal mines and steel mills of Pennsylvania. So did Italians, Russians, and Hungarians. French Canadians crossed the border and became American lumberjacks.

Into the forests went husky men from Sweden, Norway, and Germany to join Yankees and French Canadians in lumber camps. Farmers spent their winters with axe and peavey, making extra money for their families back on the land. These shanty boys were rough and hearty fellows who worked so hard felling trees, and skidding and rafting logs, that camp cooks could scarcely fill them up with sourdough bread, flapjacks, and pea soup. They lived in bunkhouses, called shanties, with big stoves in the middle of them. Of an evening tall tales were told from the "deacons' benches" and fiddles drew songs in various languages.

As the 1800's drew to their close New York City was not one, but many cities in one. Many neighborhoods were like foreign settlements, places where English was heard scarcely at all. They were called such names as Little Italy, Little Greece, Little Poland. Their people worked in clothing industries, restaurants, stores, or as carpenters and artisans.

Into California and other Pacific coast ports streamed Japanese and Chinese, to work with quiet industry on farms, gardens, and in restaurants, or laundries. America was called the Melting Pot. So many of these working people had been unable to get any education in the lands of their birth! In the United States they had a chance. When they had ability and worked hard they, or their children, could become doctors, lawyers, businessmen and women, artists, clergymen, or anything else they wished to be.

In spite of the immigration laws, with their quotas, in recent years large groups from Hungary and Cuba have been permitted to take refuge here. After the island of Puerto Rico became a self-governing commonwealth within the United States, thousands of its people crossed the water to America. Planes as well as ships bring them in every day to New York City. In the southwest, Spanish is still spoken by descendants of those Mexicans who lived there before the United States was a nation.

Along with the Indian, whose land this once was, and the Negro, brought unwillingly to our shores, all of these peoples make up America. Our leading men and women, as well as our workers, are of mixed nationalities. With the exception of the Indian, all Americans are foreign-born, or of foreign origin. Just as soon as they learn the language, and take out their papers, they become citizens. And each gives something of his own, equally valuable, to the United States of America.

UNITED STATES
TODAY

1910 AND AFTER

21 In the year 1910 Halley's comet lighted the sky as Mark Twain died. This great American writer had been born near the Mississippi River while the comet flashed across the heavens seventy-five years before. In the years between the comet's visits the United States had been divided in a Civil War, the Wild West had been explored and tamed, Americans had leveled forests and planted broad fields of corn, cotton, and hay. They had built large industries and cities into which the peoples of Europe and Asia had flocked.

After the Civil War ended there were more millionaires in America. In New York City they built mansions along Fifth Avenue, and wealthy Chicago meatpackers moved away from their city to the lakeshore where stockyards did not scent the air. General Grant became President of the United States. During his second term, in 1873, a financial panic swept the country and the whole nation suffered poverty and joblessness. By 1876, as the United States recovered, a celebration of its one hundredth year was held in Philadelphia. A World's Fair drew crowds from everywhere. On opening day the Emperor of Brazil listened to a new invention called the telephone, the work of Alexander Graham Bell, and exclaimed in amazement, "It talks!" The 1880's and 1890's saw the last battles of the Indian tribes in the West fighting bravely to hold their lands, and trying to prevent the destruction of the buffalo herds. The Spanish War, near the century's end, brought American victory and defeat to Spain in Cuba, which became independent.

Teddy Roosevelt, hero of the Spanish-American War of 1898, had been President and had cut a canal across the Isthmus of Panama. Now, in 1910, William Howard Taft was in the White House. The Alaska Gold Rush of 1897 had sent wealth into the country to pull it out of another depression. Business had grown and so had labor unions. The United States was strong, inventive, and on its way to a high position in the world. Yet, with one decade of the new century gone, it was still quiet and easygoing.

Out on the farm the family sat comfortably around their kitchen table with its one kerosene lamp. Father was reading the county newspaper, catching up on news of a farmers' organization, the Grange. He nodded as he read that the price of hay was up. Mother mended overalls, which she had scrubbed on the old washboard and cranked by hand through the wringer. Grandma bent over her tatting, and Jimmy moved his tongue across his lip as he did his sums. Susie clutched the wall telephone, which was on a party line, complaining because their neighbors would not stop talking and allow her to call her friends. There came to their ears the sound of horses stamping and cows moving in the barn. The cat edged away from the stove as old Rover stretched out his stiff legs. A lonesome locomotive whistle wailed.

Not far from the farm was the cross-roads store, with its good smells of apples, peppermint sticks, rubber boots, and cloth. In the back old men sat near the post-office cage, talking about young fellows who had gone to towns and cities. A town was a place where horses were hitched in front of stores and clapboard houses were tucked away among trees. On a Saturday night Main Street was a tight crush of people from miles around, buying, eating ice cream, or going to the picture show. A few had Victrolas and stayed home to listen to music.

Streetcars clanged in the cities, and noisy "horseless carriages" were bumping over cobbles. Their drivers, in dusters and goggles, demanded more black-topped roads for their automobiles. The nation was forging ahead with energy, but America also sat and rocked. Seven years earlier in 1903, at Kitty Hawk, N.C., the Wright brothers had launched a flimsy crate with an engine into the air. Now there were more flying machines winging away into the blue. People said those things couldn't work. But they did. "Whatever would folks think of next?" A popular saying was, "There won't be any more wars now. The world is getting civilized."

Whatever did they think of in the next half century? How did America get into the First World War in 1917? The United States, believing in the Monroe Doctrine, which was meant to keep European nations out of the Western Hemisphere, joined England and France to fight Germany. We could not accept a world ruled by German military might. Ideas and thoughts were changing rapidly. In the 1920's easygoing life took on a faster pace. Young people, in short skirts or bell-bottomed trousers, danced the Charleston and drove fast roadsters. The radio was born. As a financial depression took over the 1930's hungry, jobless people lined up before soup kitchens until President Franklin D. Roosevelt's New Deal government put them to work on government projects.

Also in the 1930's Hitler was turning Germany into ruinous ways. In 1939 he started his tanks, planes, and regiments out to conquer the world. Japan and Italy were his allies. On December 7, 1941, Japanese bombs burst without warning on the American Naval Base at Pearl Harbor, Hawaii. America mobilized to oppose Japan and Germany. The most devastating war in the history of the world burst upon the families of America. For nearly four years the United States put everything she had into defeating the Nazis, the Fascists, and the Japanese. It was remarkable that not a single city on the

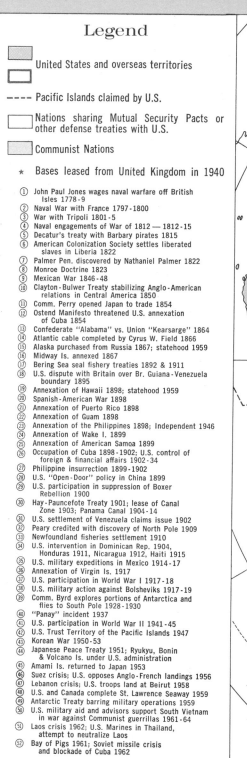

Legend

United States and overseas territories

---- Pacific Islands claimed by U.S.

Nations sharing Mutual Security Pacts or other defense treaties with U.S.

Communist Nations

★ Bases leased from United Kingdom in 1940

① John Paul Jones wages naval warfare off British Isles 1778-9
② Naval War with France 1797-1800
③ War with Tripoli 1801-5
④ Naval engagements of War of 1812 — 1812-15
⑤ Decatur's treaty with Barbary pirates 1815
⑥ American Colonization Society settles liberated slaves in Liberia 1822
⑦ Palmer Pen. discovered by Nathaniel Palmer 1822
⑧ Monroe Doctrine 1823
⑨ Mexican War 1846-48
⑩ Clayton-Bulwer Treaty stabilizing Anglo-American relations in Central America 1850
⑪ Comm. Perry opened Japan to trade 1854
⑫ Ostend Manifesto threatened U.S. annexation of Cuba 1854
⑬ Confederate "Alabama" vs. Union "Kearsarge" 1864
⑭ Atlantic cable completed by Cyrus W. Field 1866
⑮ Alaska purchased from Russia 1867; statehood 1959
⑯ Midway Is. annexed 1867
⑰ Bering Sea seal fishery treaties 1892 & 1911
⑱ U.S. dispute with Britain over Br. Guiana-Venezuela boundary 1895
⑲ Annexation of Hawaii 1898; statehood 1959
⑳ Spanish-American War 1898
㉑ Annexation of Puerto Rico 1898
㉒ Annexation of Guam 1898
㉓ Annexation of the Philippines 1898; Independent 1946
㉔ Annexation of Wake I. 1899
㉕ Annexation of American Samoa 1899
㉖ Occupation of Cuba 1898-1902; U.S. control of foreign & financial affairs 1902-34
㉗ Philippine insurrection 1899-1902
㉘ U.S. "Open-Door" policy in China 1899
㉙ U.S. participation in suppression of Boxer Rebellion 1900
㉚ Hay-Pauncefote Treaty 1901; lease of Canal Zone 1903; Panama Canal 1904-14
㉛ U.S. settlement of Venezuela claims issue 1902
㉜ Peary credited with discovery of North Pole 1909
㉝ Newfoundland fisheries settlement 1910
㉞ U.S. intervention in Dominican Rep. 1904, Honduras 1911, Nicaragua 1912, Haiti 1915
㉟ U.S. military expeditions in Mexico 1914-17
㊱ Annexation of Virgin Is. 1917
㊲ U.S. participation in World War I 1917-18
㊳ U.S. military action against Bolsheviks 1917-19
㊴ Comm. Byrd explores portions of Antarctica and flies to South Pole 1928-1930
㊵ "Panay" incident 1937
㊶ U.S. participation in World War II 1941-45
㊷ U.S. Trust Territory of the Pacific Islands 1947
㊸ Korean War 1950-53
㊹ Japanese Peace Treaty 1951; Ryukyu, Bonin & Volcano Is. under U.S. administration
㊺ Amami Is. returned to Japan 1953
㊻ Suez crisis; U.S. opposes Anglo-French landings 1956
㊼ Lebanon crisis; U.S. troops land at Beirut 1958
㊽ U.S. and Canada complete St. Lawrence Seaway 1959
㊾ Antarctic Treaty barring military operations 1959
㊿ U.S. military aid and advisors support South Vietnam in war against Communist guerrillas 1961-64
51 Laos crisis 1962; U.S. Marines in Thailand, attempt to neutralize Laos
52 Bay of Pigs 1961; Soviet missile crisis and blockade of Cuba 1962

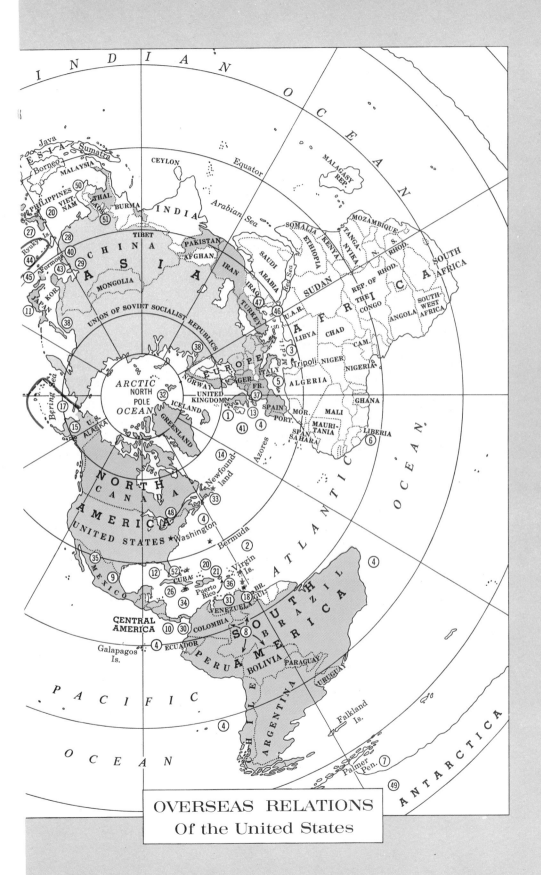

INDIAN OCEAN

Java
Sumatra
Borneo
MALAYSIA
ESIA
CEYLON
Equator
MALAGASY REP.

PHILIPPINES
VIET NAM
THAI.
BURMA
INDIA
Arabian Sea
SOMALIA
MOZAMBIQUE
KENYA
TANGA-
NYIKA
N.S.
RHOD.
SOUTH AFRICA

⑳
㊿
㉗
㉘
㊿
⑪

TIBET
PAKISTAN
AFGHAN.
SAUDI
ARABIA
ETHIOPIA
SUDAN
REP. OF RHOD.
THE I
CONGO
RHOD.
SOUTH-WEST AFRICA

ASIA
CHINA
⑳
㊵
㉙
㊸
㊺
JAP. KOR.
Formosa

MONGOLIA
IRAN
IRAQ
TURKEY
㊼
㊻
U.A.R.
Red Sea
LIBYA
CHAD
NIGER
CAM.
NIGERIA
ANGOLA
AFRICA

UNION OF SOVIET SOCIALIST REPUBLICS

㊳
㊳

EUROPE
NORWAY
GER.
ITALY
FR.
⑤
Tripoli
Med.
ALGERIA
GHANA

ARCTIC
NORTH POLE
OCEAN
㉜
ICELAND
UNITED KINGDOM
㊲
SPAIN
PORT.
MOR.
SPAN.
SAHARA
MALI
MAURI-TANIA
LIBERIA

Bering Sea
⑰
⑮
U.S.
ALASKA
GREENLAND
①
⑬
④
⑥

NORTH
CANADA
⑭
Newfound-land
⑬
Azores

AMERICA
UNITED STATES ★Washington
㊽
㉝
④
Bermuda
②

MEXICO
⑨
㉟
⑫
㊿
⑳
㉑
Virgin Is.
㊱
Puerto Rico
⑱
BR. GUI.
④
ATLANTIC

CENTRAL
AMERICA
⑩
㉚
COLOMBIA
VENEZUELA
㉛
⑧
BRAZIL
SOUTH
AMERICA
OCEAN

Galapagos Is.
④
ECUADOR
PERU
BOLIVIA
PARAGUAY
④

PACIFIC
④
CHILE
ARGENTINA
URUGUAY
Falkland Is.

OCEAN
Palmer Pen.
⑦
⑲
ANTARCTICA

OVERSEAS RELATIONS
Of the United States

☆ 119

U.S. mainland was bombed.

American troops landed in Italy, and then the greatest invasion force ever assembled on earth came ashore on the French coast of Normandy. A vast armada of American and British ships emptied troops, vehicles, and weapons onto the beaches, under ravaging fire, while the sky was black with planes bombarding the Germans inland. The United States fought alongside England and France, and Russia defended her homeland from Hitler on the eastern front. From island to island in the Pacific American soldiers, sailors, and marines battled the Japanese. The United States sent twelve million men into the conflict in the second World War. Toward the end of these war years Franklin D. Roosevelt died and Harry Truman became President. At the conclusion of the struggle America was a world leader. She had also used a new weapon on the Japanese. This was the atomic bomb, developed here after leading scientists had told President Roosevelt that Germany was about to make a nuclear bomb.

The Nuclear Age began, and so did the cold war between two kinds of governments, capitalist and communist. After 1945, the only nation challenging the power of America was the Soviet Union. Nuclear energy could be used for peaceful as well as military purposes, but both the United States and Russia made larger and more destructive bombs. Until a treaty banning nuclear explosions in the atmosphere was signed in 1963, both governments were setting off explosions that dropped nuclear fallout into the air. Swept by winds across the globe, poison fell upon the earth.

Americans looked at wide-screen movies, or watched television. Electricity made many things possible, even on farms and in distant places. The countryside sprouted enormous steel towers to carry the electricity. Ruthless bulldozers and earth movers cut wide swaths through farms, towns, and cities making turnpikes, expressways, and thruways. On these super highways long lines of trucks and cars moved endlessly. Lights — white, yellow, red, and green — turned the night skies into man-made reflectors.

Father nodded over his newspaper telling of "brush-fire" wars in distant places with strange names. Mother sat down to watch television while machines did her washing and drying. Granny fluffed her blue-white hair under an electrically heated hood, and Bobby, in the next room, played hootenanny music on his hi-fi as he studied his lessons. Debbie, wearing stretch pants and sweater, took complete possession of the telephone for the evening. Overhead jet planes zoomed, rocking the house with sonic booms. The dog and the cat retired together to the far end of the cellar.

Everything came close to one's life. Everything was ready-made. Everything was "instant." And people were saying, "There will not be another war. Because, if there is, nuclear bombs will wipe all life from the face of the earth. There can't be another great war!"

WHAT LIES AHEAD?

Since the first voyage of Columbus people have journeyed to America hoping for many things. They wanted to find the Northwest Passage to the Orient. They came to look for treasure in gold and jewels. They sought new lives and new homes, prosperity, education, and religious freedom. They made the United States so large that, with Alaska and Hawaii added in 1959, fifty stars appeared on Old Glory.

People came alone or in little groups. They swarmed ashore in great waves of immigration from everywhere. All over the world America was called a young nation — a New World. The United States does not seem so young now. There are many newer, although smaller, countries in Africa, Asia, and the Middle East.

For centuries America drew people into itself. Now we are sending Americans out to other lands. Our young men and women go to army, naval, air force and missile bases around the globe. Since our food and industrial production is the greatest in the world, we also send out experts to administer aid programs for other countries. We take part in the work of the United Nations helping children, giving medical care and agricultural instruction.

Just a short time ago church missionaries were the only men and women from Western nations going out to help other peoples without trying to extend military power, or make money. Now the *Hope* ship sails from the United States to South America to give medical treatment, and to train doctors and nurses of these less developed countries to help their own people more efficiently. Young men and women volunteer for the Peace Corps. They go to far corners of the world. This government program is based on teaching and helping those who need it.

There are teachers and students who travel to foreign countries in exchange for others who come to America. Our cultural exchange program takes artists, theatrical performers, sports teams, scientists, and technicians abroad.

America is no longer far away from the older countries. Speed has telescoped time and space. Although the automobile was first developed in Europe, within the lifetime of one man it made almost a complete change in the life of America. Before 1914, the driver of one of those "speed demon autos" could go at a frightening pace of fifteen miles an hour on a good road. He was hated by anyone who owned a horse. By 1920, the speed limit on a paved road was actually twenty-five miles an hour! On superhighways of the 1960's cars travel legally at sixty miles an hour, and a driver is likely to report a slowpoke to a state trooper.

In their early days railroad trains traveled at a dizzy speed of eighteen miles an hour. Soon it was sixty — seventy — eighty miles an hour! Now express trains roar through the countryside with Diesel engine horns braying like Missouri mules. Old-timers miss the lonely voice of the steam locomotive. Early sailing ships took months to cross the Atlantic Ocean. With the coming of steam they made the crossing in weeks. Now a big liner speeds from New York to England in three or four days.

Airplanes make time a confusing thing. A traveler can leave New York by nonstop jet plane at breakfast time and arrive more than 3,000 miles away in San Francisco five hours later. Just in time for lunch, too! Often a passenger must rush to finish a meal in the air before he has to get off the plane. He may have to spend more time in a traffic snarl on the highway going to the airport than he does on the flight. More than an hour can easily pass driving from home to New York City, or one of its suburbs, to the Kennedy Airport. And yet the traveler will spend no more than forty minutes actually in the air on his way to Boston. Some transatlantic jets cross the ocean to Europe at speeds of 500 miles an hour. In the 1960's marvels come thick and fast.

What seems miraculous to us today? The Russian Sputnik, first satellite to orbit the earth, has been followed by others sent up by both the United States and the Soviet Union. The first passenger in a Russian rocket was a dog. In America it was a monkey. Americans and Russians have orbited the earth. One thrilling day Americans could not take their eyes from the television screen as John Glenn, astronaut, whizzed at incredible speed into orbit in his space capsule. That journey has been made by others who also returned to earth safely, including a Russian woman astronaut. What comes next in the Space Age? Perhaps, before long, men and women will land on the moon.

Scientists are doing remarkable things with electricity, with nuclear experiments in medicine, and with miracle drugs. The business world has electronic computers — those fantastic, non-human calculators! Automation is doing the job of many men in industrial plants, and even in the United States Post Office.

And yet, with man's head stretched upward as his eyes try to follow the flight of missiles, rockets, and astronauts, there are enormous problems on earth that he has not solved. Relations with other nations are complicated and difficult. In prosperous America there are miserable slums and increasing crimes. Not every disease has been conquered. Automatic machines put men out of work and worry labor. Schools are overcrowded and need more teachers. Negroes can no longer wait until some future time to be equal in the rights of citizens, as the American Constitution guarantees.

To early man the shape of his world was only the circle that he could see around him as he turned his eyes to follow the sun in the course of one clear day. Then he enlarged his view of the earth to fit the distant places where he had been and could remember. He grew brave enough to imagine without fear of the unknown. He learned to read and his world expanded in his thoughts to places that he had never seen. After Christopher Columbus sailed his little fleet to the west and Ferdinand Magellan circumnavigated the globe, a man knew that the world was not a flat disk floating among clouds. He began to realize that the universe did not revolve just for him. His world was no larger than the earth, and the earth was only a speck of dust in the universe.

Today the world in our minds is bounded by nothing on the earth itself. We know the earth to be a globe, not quite completely round in shape, with continents, oceans, islands, and polar regions to the north and south. There are still challenging unknown places for men and women to explore. There are mountains to climb and valleys, jungles and streams to see for the first time. But man's mind also ventures into the realm of the unknown — into space itself. He realizes that his knowledge of the universe is imperfect, but he will extend it. A man is a wanderer! He is a searcher! He wants to learn what is just beyond the expanding world that he knows, or has imagined. And then he tries to go there!

INDEX

MAP INDEX